MEDIA, FEMINISM, CULTURAL STUDIES

Stepping Forward: Essays, Lectures and Interviews
by Wolfgang Iser

Wild Zones: Pornography, Art and Feminism
by Kelly Ives

Global Media Warning: Explorations of Radio, Television and the Press
by Oliver Whitehorne

'Cosmo Woman': The World of Women's Magazines
by Oliver Whitehorne

Andrea Dworkin
by Jeremy Mark Robinson

Cixous, Irigaray, Kristeva: The Jouissance of French Feminism
by Kelly Ives

Sex in Art: Pornography and Pleasure in Painting and Sculpture
by Cassidy Hughes

*The Erotic Object: Sexuality in Sculpture
From Prehistory to the Present Day*
by Susan Quinnell

Women in Pop Music
by Helen Challis

Detonation Britain: Nuclear War in the UK
by Jeremy Mark Robinson

Julia Kristeva: Art, Love, Melancholy, Philosophy, Semiotics
by Kelly Ives

Luce Irigaray: Lips, Kissing, and the Politics of Sexual Difference
by Kelly Ives

Helene Cixous I Love You: The Jouissance of Writing
by Kelly Ives

The Poetry of Cinema
by John Madden

The Sacred Cinema of Andrei Tarkovsky
by Jeremy Mark Robinson

Disney Business, Disney Films, Disney Lands
Daniel Cerruti

Feminism and Shakespeare
by B.D. Barnacle

Thomas Hardy's *Tess of the d'Urbervilles*
A Critical Study

THOMAS HARDY'S
Tess of the d'Urbervilles

A Critical Study

MARGARET ELVY

CRESCENT MOON

First published 2000. Second edition 2008. Third edition 2012.
© Margaret Elvy 2000, 2008, 2012.

Printed and bound in the U.S.A.
Set in Book Antiqua 10 on 14pt and Gill Sans display.
Designed by Radiance Graphics.

The right of Margaret Elvy to be identified as the author of *Thomas Hardy's Tess of the d'Urbervilles* has been asserted generally in accordance with sections 77 and 78 of the Copyright, Designs and Patents Act 1988.

All rights reserved. No part of this book may be reprinted or reproduced, stored in a retrieval system, or transmitted, in any form or by any means, electronic, mechanical, photocopying, recording or otherwise, without permission from the publisher.

British Library Cataloguing in Publication data

Elvy, Margaret
Thomas Hardy's Tess of the d'Urbervilles: A Critical Study. –
(Thomas Hardy Studies Series; v. 5)
1. Hardy, Thomas, 1840-1928. Tess of the d'Urbervilles
I. Title
823.8

ISBN-13 9781861713872 (Pbk)
ISBN-13 9781861713704 (Hbk)

CRESCENT MOON PUBLISHING
P.O. Box 1312, Maidstone
Kent, ME14 5XU, Great Britain
www.crmoon.com

CONTENTS

Abbreviations   9

1 Introductory: The Thomas Hardy Myth   15
2 Thomas Hardy and Feminism   21
3 'Lie or Die': *Tess of the d'Urbervilles*   69

Illustrations   151
Notes   159
Bibliography   167

ABBREVIATIONS

J	*Jude the Obscure*
T	*Tess of the D'Urbervilles*
R	*The Return of the Native*
W	*The Woodlanders*
M	*The Mayor of Casterbridge*
F	*Far From the Madding Crowd*
U	*Under the Greenwood Tree*
PBE	*A Pair of Blue Eyes*
WB	*The Well-Beloved*
TT	*Two on a Tower*
Lao	*A Laocidean*
DR	*Desperate Remedies*
HE	*The Hand of Ethelberta*
TM	*The Trumpet-Major*
D	*The Dynasts*
CP	*Complete Poems*
Love	*Hardy's Love Poems*
SS	*The Short Stories of Thomas Hardy*
Lit	*The Literary Notebooks of Thomas Hardy*
Let	*The Collected Letters of Thomas Hardy*
Per	*The Personal Notebooks of Thomas Hardy*
L	*The Life and Work of Thomas Hardy*
PW	*Personal Writings*
H	*The Sense of Sex*, ed. Margaret Higonnet

Thomas Hardy's *Tess of the d'Urbervilles*
A Critical Study

O world! O life! O time!
On whose last steps I climb,
Trembling at that where I had stood before;
When will return the glory of your prime?
No more – Oh, never more!

Percy Bysshe Shelley, 'A Lament'

Thomas Hardy (courtesy of Dorset County Museum)

Marnhull in Dorset, maybe an inspiration for Marlott in *Tess* (Dorset County Museum)

1

Introductory:
The Thomas Hardy Myth

A mass of critical data has grown up around Thomas Hardy. He is one of the most discussed authors in the English language. This sample from critic John Peck (in *How to Study a Thomas Hardy Novel*) is typical of the kind of Hardy criticism which sees in his work a marvellous evocation of hidden emotions, often vaguely called the unconscious:

> *Hardy offers us something more exciting than a mirror image of life... he always writes with a sense of a force which is elusive and cannot be explained... his most extraordinary ability is to create and convey a sense of a natural energy at work in life.* (59)

One could also cite Thomas Hardy critics such as Ian Gregor, John Bayley, Michael Millgate, Merryn Williams, Jean Brooks, Arnold Kettle, Irving Howe, David Cecil, Philip Larkin, W.H.

Auden and a host of others as producing similar criticism. Hardy has had it easy, as far as most criticism is concerned. The collections of essays and criticism (such as those edited by Albert Guerard, Anne Smith, Albert J. LaValley, Dale Kramer, Harold Bloom, Norman Page, R.P. Draper and Phillip Mallett, the stalwarts of any public or college library), were sincere efforts, but hardly ever offered something other than humanist, formal, and often vague criticism. Even in the 1980s and 1990s books on Thomas Hardy kept coming out which preferred not to acknowledge cultural theory writers and philosophers such as Jacques Derrida, Gilles Deleuze, Felix Guattari, Paul de Man, Jean Baudrillard, Mikhail Bakhtin, Jacques Lacan, Annette Kuhn and Laura Mulvey, or feminist thinkers such as Julia Kristeva, Luce Irigaray, Gayatri Chakravorty Spivak, Linda Williams, Monique Wittig, Adrienne Rich, Alice Jardine, bell hooks, Judith Butler, Teresa de Lauretis and Elizabeth Grosz.

The two most perceptive collections of essays on Thomas Hardy up to the mid-1990s were edited by Lance St John Butler (*Alternative Hardy*, 1989) and Margaret Higonnet (*The Sense of Sex: Feminist Perspectives on Hardy*, 1993). After Jacques Derrida and deconstruction, to take one kind of post-1960s criticism, texts were no longer 'whole', but were, in the words of an important Hardy critic (J. Hillis Miller), 'undecidable'. Texts were 'self-subverting', in the process of dismantling themselves, leading to a multiplicity of sometimes conflicting readings.[1] As a mid-1990s book of feminist criticism said (*Gendering the Reader*), a heterogeneity of theoretical positions seems to be inevitable (S. Mills, 1993, 283).

Where critics have a field day demolishing Thomas Hardy's art is in his literary style in his fiction. Hardy's prose style at its worst is marked by 'verbosity and redundance, with ponderous words, clumsily polysyllabic, and unhappy phrases' (I. Baker, 95). Hardy's deliberate complexity or learned allusions do sometimes make his fiction very creaky and ugly. Occasionally, he *is* really bad, so the reader cringes. Often the failures in style occur in lulls between events, because when some dramatic event is taking place, such as the storm over the ricks in *Far From the Madding Crowd*, Hardy's narration is tremendous (but then, only a terrible writer couldn't make a storm work in writing). (Peter Widdowson has noted some of Hardy's flaws: a propensity for melodrama; over-use of chance/ coincidence; pessimism; tendency towards implausibility and improbability; and 'his at times pedantic, awkward, mannered style' [1993, 5]).

Thomas Hardy divided up his novels into three groups, and Hardy critics have kept, by and large, to the divisions ever since. The six 'great'/ 'tragic' Hardy novels are *Tess of the d'Urbervilles, Jude the Obscure, The Return of the Native, The Mayor of Casterbridge, Far From the Madding Crowd* and *The Woodlanders*. This is the central group of novels that is discussed in nearly every book on Hardy. It corresponds to Hardy's 'Novels of Character and Environment'. Hardy criticism next groups together the 'minor' or 'secondary' novels, which come from the category 'Romances and Fantasies': *Two On a Tower, A Pair of Blue Eyes, The Trumpet-Major, The Well-Beloved* and *Under the Greenwood Tree* (this latter is in Hardy's first group, though hardly any Hardy critic puts it beside *Tess* or *Jude*). This middle group of 'lesser' novels is usually discussed in Tom Hardy criticism, often dealt with in one chapter, with the major novels having a chapter each. The short stories are usually analyzed in the 'minor works' chapter: *Life's Little Ironies, Wessex Tales* and *A Group of Noble Dames*. Then come the novels which are rarely discussed anywhere: *The Hand of Ethelberta, Desperate Remedies* and *A Laodicean*. It is assumed (wrongly, perhaps) that the 'lesser' novels, such as *A Laodicean* and *Desperate Remedies*, have too many faults to make them 'great' or worthy of discussion.

Many of the books on Thomas Hardy's fiction stay safe and discuss his Wessex world, or his nature poetry, the 'Thomas Hardy' of a rural, nostalgic and now lost world (Denys Kay-Robinson, Hermann Lea, Merryn Williams, W. Sherren, W.J. Keith, John Alcorn, and B.A.C. Windle). In this view, 'Hardy' is the 'tragic novelist of character struggling heroically with Nature,

Fate, or other, pre-eminently non-social forces' (P. Widdowson, 1983, 13). This is the 'Thomas Hardy' the tourist and TV industries promulgate, the 'Thomas Hardy' of prestige television adaptions and tourist board brochures. Hélène Cixous writes that 'the mystery is that we confuse invent and believe.'[2] This is worth keeping in mind, especially with regard to Hardy's characters, who seem so 'real', so that Hardy fans, visiting modern-day Marnhull in North Dorset, think they are beholding Tess Durbeyfield's 'real' cottage. (The most well-known film version of *Tess* is probably the 1979 movie starring Natassja Kinski. There have also been many stage, TV and radio adaptions – it's a favourite book for British TV, theatre and radio, for instance; some are included here in the illustrations).

Much of Thomas Hardy criticism is of the humanist, formal, New Criticism ilk, taking Hardy's texts as the products of one person (Irving Howe, J.I.M. Stewart, David Cecil, John Bayley, Lascelles Abercrombie, Virginia Woolf, Denys Kay-Robinson, Jean Brooks, Michael Millgate, F.B. Pinion, A. Alvarez, Simon Gatrell, R.P. Draper, Robert Schweik, J.W. Beach, Edmund Blunden, Donald Davie, Merryn Williams, Ian Gregor and Albert Guerard). These were the critics that helped elevate Hardy into the centre of English literature. Few critics had anything new to say about Hardy's fiction that had not already been said by the 1950s.

Thomas Hardy has had one or two critics that have produced startling work, the most obvious is perhaps D.H. Lawrence, whose *A Study of Thomas Hardy* has provoked much critical debate. Indeed, there is a section of Hardy (meta)criticism devoted to Lawrence on Hardy.

It was surprising, perhaps, that F.R. Leavis left Thomas Hardy out of his Great Tradition. It is odd that Leavis exalted George Eliot and D.H. Lawrence, but not Thomas Hardy. Leavis grudgingly acknowledged the greatness of a dozen of Hardy's poems, but his novels were vastly overrated, Leavis reckoned.[3] Hardy's work, though, had far too many other critics championing it to be much affected by Leavis's omission.

Another 'Thomas Hardy' beloved of critics is the philosopher, pessimist and sometime Buddhist (authors such as H. Garwood, H.B. Grimsditch, Lance St John Butler, P. Braybrooke, Ralph W.W. Elliott, F.R. Southerington, E.J. Brennecke, G.W. Sherman and Jagdish Chandra Dave have written of Hardy's philosophy). This is the 'Thomas Hardy' that became an Existentialist in the 1950s, an inheritor of the German philosophy of Arthur Schopenhauer and Friedrich Nietzsche, a dramatist in the Theatre of the Absurd of Eugene Ionesco, Antonin Artaud and Samuel Beckett.

Thomas Hardy's biographers have not greatly altered his critical status, whether the biographies have been 'sympathetic' (Michael Millgate, R.L. Purdy, Timothy O'Sullivan, Carl J. Weber, F.B. Pinion, and F. Halliday), or seen as potentially damaging (Martin Seymour-Smith, and Robert Gittings). There have been too few critical views of Hardy's works that use materialism, Marxism, deconstructionism, psychoanalysis, semiotics, feminism or postmodernism. Critics who have employed some of the more recent critical approaches, loosely termed 'cultural theory', include J. Hillis Miller, Lance St John Butler, John Goode, Roger Ebbatson, J.-J. Lecercle, R. Saldivar, Terry Eagleton, Peter Widdowson, Janie Sénéchal-Teissedou, Charles Lock, Tony Tanner and George Wootton. Critics I would cite as particularly enriching, not including the feminist critics (see below), include Widdowson, Lecercle, Lawrence and Goode, and to a lesser extent, Ebbatson, Tanner and Eagleton.

One might suppose that Tom Hardy's work has been particularly well-served by feminist criticism – there seems to have been a lot of it (Penny Boumelha, Virginia Woolf, Patricia Stubbs, Katherine Rogers, Elaine Showalter, Rosalind Miles, Rosemarie Morgan, Rosemary Sumner, Patricia Ingham, T.R. Wright, Mary Jacobus, Kate Millett, Linda Williams and Marjorie Garson). 'Probably no male author in English literature has been the subject of so much feminist appraisal', wrote Charles Lock in

Thomas Hardy: Criticism in Focus (126). I would disagree: D.H. Lawrence has had just as much attention from feminists, and Lawrence feminist criticism has generally been of a higher quality. Ditto with William Shakespeare.

Feminist critics have been interested by the feminism-in-the-making in Thomas Hardy's fiction, and by his female characters.[4] Hardy says a lot about the human, and feminine predicament. His texts manage, through an impressionist approach, to make people 'enlarged and dignified', as Virginia Woolf put it. Hardy's ability to dignify and elevate people is partly what makes him 'the greatest tragic writer among English novelists' (1932, 253f).

Much of Thomas Hardy criticism is masculinist and bound to a gendered approach, like most literary criticism from the ancient Greeks onwards. However, except in a few cases (Mary Jacobus, Kaja Silverman, Kathleen Blake, Elisabeth Bronfen, Dianne Fallon Sadoff, Linda Williams and Rosemarie Morgan), most feminist Hardy criticism is usually of the well-trodden second wave (1960s-1980s) feminist type, as epitomized by Kate Millett's *Sexual Politics*. Laudable as the attempts of most feminist critics are, their insights into Hardy's work remain limited and disappointing (Rosemary Sumner, Rosalind Miles, Elaine Showalter, Penny Boumelha, Patricia Stubbs, Katherine Rogers and Patricia Ingham). Far and away the best collection of feminist approaches to Hardy's work, and one of the very best books on Hardy, is *The Sense of Sex* (edited by Margaret Higonnet, 1993).

2

Thomas Hardy and Feminism

> *What are my books but one long plea against 'man's inhumanity to man' – to woman – and to the lower animals? Whatever may be the inherent good or evil of life, it is certain that men make it much worse than it need be.*
>
> Thomas Hardy, 1904 (in F. Pinion, 1968, 178)

Is Thomas Hardy (a) feminist? Are Thomas Hardy's works feminist? How much do his works reflect and bolster the patriarchal attitudes and values of his era, and how much do they question them? Does Hardy employ feminist approaches to the society he lives in? What is the relation between Hardy and the feminists of his time? And what is the relation between Hardy's works and the feminism of the early 21st century? These are interrelated questions. We are concerned here with Thomas Hardy's novels, not the man or author himself, and the fiction's relations with contemporary feminism. When we write Thomas Hardy we mean the 'Thomas Hardy' that is written into the novels, the 'Thomas Hardy' who is and is not the narrator of the novels.¹ We mean the 'Thomas Hardy' created by the texts, not the biographical, 'real' 'Thomas Hardy' who lived at Max Gate in Dorchester, who had certain literary and wealthy friends, who went up to London for 'the season', who bicycled around Dorset, who was fond of pet dogs (the 'Thomas Hardy' evoked in the *Life*, Hardy's autobiography).

Instead of there being a direct connection between author and reader, which humanist criticism assumes, there can be seen to be at least six levels of mediation: real author > implied author > narrator > narratee > implied reader > real reader.² The 'real reader' is thus at a critical distance from the 'real author', 'Thomas Hardy'. One has to consider, as well as the author, exactly what (a) character is – a function of the text? What is the relation between character and text? A character is interpreted differently by everyone: how is a character constructed in the minds of different readers? What are the factors, 'inside' and 'outside' the text, that govern character?

Thomas Hardy's theme is 'Wessexuality', 'Wes-sex-mania', Wes-sexual politics. Thomas Hardy's works are, for feminists, sexist, patriarchal and masculinist, and yet they question notions of sexism, gender, identity, subjectivity, patriarchy and masculinism.³ A text such as 1891's *Tess of the d'Urbervilles* is 'traditional', and follows patriarchal codes and morals. Yet it also questions them, and offers a number of (feminist) critiques of late 19th century society. In his letters, Hardy proposed feminist views; he wrote to feminists such as the suffragette leader Millicent Fawcett that a child was the mother's own business, not the father's (*Collected Letters*, 3, 238).

One can see these feminist sentiments in, for example, Thomas Hardy's treatment of Tess Durbeyfield in her motherhood: she works in the fields just a few weeks after the birth, even though she is melancholy (she seems to be suffering a mild form of post-natal depression). Tess further subverts the patriarchy of the times in Great Britain by taking her child's baptism into her own hands. She goes against her father, the vicar, and the whole church with her self-made baptism.

Donald Hall offers a typical (male) critical response to *Tess of the d'Urbervilles*: 'Hardy was clearly in love with Tess, and he leaves his male readers in the same condition.'[4] What a ridiculous comment! Rosalind Miles' view of Hardy and women is typical of the second wave (1960s-1908s) feminist criticism ('womanist' is a better term) which was pro-Hardy. For Miles (in "The Women of Wessex"), Hardy had an intuitive and exalted view of women:

> *He had, surely, a deeply intuitive understanding of female nature... Hardy's guileless and ecstatic response to women in life irradiated his writing at every possible level... For Hardy really is a lover of women in the fullest physical sense.* (1979, 25-26)

For some feminists, Thomas Hardy did not necessarily 'like' women, as (male) critics such as Irving Howe claimed (M. Childers, 1981).

A typical second wave feminist analysis of Thomas Hardy's work comes from Elaine Showalter. In "Towards a Feminist Poetics" (1979), Showalter offers a rather simplistic analysis of the famous wife-selling scene in *The Mayor of Casterbridge* (a gift to feminists). Showalter takes as her departure point one of the archetypal humanist studies of Hardy, Irving Howe's *Thomas Hardy* (1968).

> *What Howe, like other male critics of Hardy, conveniently overlooks about the novel is that Henchard sells not only his wife but his child, a child who can only be female. Patriarchal societies do not readily sell their sons, but their daughters are all for sale sooner or later.* (in M. Jacobus, 1979, 26f)

Elaine Showalter's feminist analysis is in the same sort of vein as the feminism in Kate Millett's *Sexual Politics*. Millett's 1970 book deconstructed writers such as Henry Miller, Norman Mailer and D.H. Lawrence, exposing the sexist assumptions in their books. Millett's analysis, though (which I find irritatingly simplistic and reductionist), like much of Anglo-American feminism, is distinctly humanist, and modernist, assuming that whatever is in the text relates *directly* to the author, that whatever is in the text is there deliberately and consciously, placed there by the author her/himself. This kind of Anglo-American feminism assumes that the text is transparent, so that if a text appears misogynist, then that writer is misogynist.

French feminism, cultural studies and postmodern feminism, however, does not regard the text as transparent, and departs dramatically from humanist criticism at many key points. Humanist feminism talks of Thomas Hardy, but postmodern or cultural theory feminism talks of 'Thomas Hardy', that is, a writer who is 'written' by the social, ideological, cultural, materialist and economic forces around him. Feminism of the type of Kate Millett, Elaine Showalter, Rosalind Miles *et al* essentializes Hardy's female characters: this view of Miles' is typical: '[f]or Hardy, femininity was a value, an essence, an eternal and inescapable fact' (1979, 43), which's patently untrue. Showalter's Anglo-American feminist analysis, meanwhile, is strong on simple assertions, but short on subtle, ironic, thoughtful insights. Showalter, for example, asserts:

> Hardy's female characters in The Mayor of Casterbridge, *as in his other novels, are somewhat idealised and melancholy projections of a repressed male self.* (ib., 26f)

Elaine Showalter assumes a direct line back from the character to the author. Roland Barthes called for the 'death of the author', where the idea of the author who suffers for the book, who 'nourishes' the book, is discarded in favour of a notion of writing as a 'multi-dimensional space in which a variety of writings, none of them original, blend and clash' (1984, 144f). In cultural theory, 'writing' or 'literature' is multi-dimensional, with an infinity of possible readings. Linearity is discarded, and texts continually change. Nothing is fixed anymore, and meanings fluctuate.

Thomas Hardy's women characters are known and yet not known – by the reader (and, one suspects, by the narrator). Rather than getting to know the women figures in Hardy's novels, the reader gets to know Hardy's narrator (but not Hardy himself).[5] Female characters such as Tess, Eustacia, Sue and Bathsheba, seem to have a substantial and subtle subjectivity, but, as Judith Mitchell argues, their subjecthood is 'largely illusory' (ib., 179). Hardy's narrators offer detailed physical descriptions of the female characters, but leave out much of their thoughts. This is part of Hardy's narrational project, but it can also be seen as 'a glaring omission of female consciousness' (ib., 183). Hardy, via his narrators, gets up close and lovingly describes his heroines' physical features (most obviously, in *Tess of the d'Urbervilles*, Tess's body), but his narrators are also oddly distanced from his characters. Consequently, Hardy's heroines remain mysterious, always partially unknowable by the reader.

There are moments, for example, when the reader would expect to find out what a female character is thinking: when Eustacia Vye is wandering the Heath just before her death in *The Return of the Native*, or Tess's feelings after she has killed Alec d'Urberville. Even in more mundane, less dramatic moments, such as when Marty puts down her billhook at the beginning of *The Woodlanders* and looks at her blistered hand, when the reader might expect to find out what she is thinking, the narrative moves into a more general voice.[6]

Patricia Stubbs pointed out in *Women and Fiction: Feminism and the Novel, 1880-1920* that Thomas Hardy was ambivalent about his female characters, not always condemning the social pressures and psychological characteristics that contributed towards women's suffering (1979, 81f). Penny Boumelha reckoned in *Thomas Hardy and Women: Sexual Ideology and Narrative* that the radicalism of Hardy's depictions of women did not reside in their 'complexity' or 'realism' but 'in their resistance to a single and uniform ideological position' (1982, 7).

Thomas Hardy's novels were not always received favourably by women critics and readers. Hardy's own views, expressed outside of the novels, did not always square with those of feminists of the 1880s and 1890s. The ideological gap between

Hardy and the women critics and feminists of the late 19th century is illustrated by Hardy's remark to Edmund Yates (in 1891): 'many of my novels have suffered so much from misrepresentation as being attacks on womankind.' (*Collected Letters*, I, 250) Hardy hoped that works such as *Tess of the d'Urbervilles* would redress the balance.

In Tom Hardy's fiction, as in so much of modern literature (certainly in the works of James Joyce, Norman Mailer, Henry Miller, D.H. Lawrence, Virginia Woolf, Gertrude Stein and J.P. Donleavy), women and men are at odds with each other. The connection between men and women in fiction is always fraught with conflict. Luce Irigaray suggests a fundamental *difference* between the sexes:

> *Man and woman, woman and man are therefore always meeting as though for the first time since they cannot stand in for one another. I shall never take the place of a man, never will a man take mine.*[7]

A politics of sexual union between men and women has still not been created, Irigaray suggests, because there is no continuity between the spiritual and material, the sacred and the sexual aspects of life.

However, at an artistic and novelistic level, it is a commonplace of all drama to generate continual conflicts: thus, in Hardy's fiction, it's not only men and women who struggle against each other, it's women and women, men and men, parents and children, people and society, people and industry, people and capitalism, whatever.

THOMAS HARDY AND SEXUAL DIFFERENCE

Lesbian, gay and queer cultural theory has continually addressed the problem of identity and gender (increasingly since the 1960s). There are certain sexual and social 'positions' or 'categories' which are seen as 'outside' the (patriarchal) (Western) norms, which may have affinities with the female 'outsider' figures of French feminists Julia Kristeva and Luce Irigaray. The lesbian, for instance, is sometimes seen as an 'outsider', like the black woman, or the feminist. Gender and sexual identity categories are becoming increasingly blurred. For example, there are 'physical' lesbians, 'natural' lesbians, 'cultural' or 'social' lesbians, and 'male' lesbians (men who culturally position themselves as lesbians). There are men with vaginas and women with penises; there are queer butches and aggressive femmes, there are F2Ms and lesbians who love men, queer queens and drag kings, daddy boys and dyke mummies, transsexual Asians, butch bottoms, femme tops, women and lesbians who fuck men, women and lesbians who fuck *like* men, bull daggers, lesbians who dress up as men impersonating women, lesbians who dress up as straight men in order to pick up gay men, butches who dress in fem clothing to feel like a gay man dressing as a woman, femmes butched-out in male drag and butches femmed-out in drag. Sexual and social identities are continually being performed, blurred, re-defined, questioned. Terms such as 'straight' and 'gay', hetero and homo/ hommo, are no longer adequate for these multi-layered, postmodern sexual identities. As Judith Halberstam puts it '[w]e are all transsexuals'.[8]

Some feminists regard sexuality as expressed through performances and gestures, rather than being some essence or some given. Thus heterosexuality itself is not an unchanging 'institution', but may already be a 'constant parody of itself', as Judith Butler suggests in *Gender Trouble: Feminism and the Subversion of Identity* (1990, 122). Heterosexuality, Butler reckons, is continually imitating itself, always miming its own performances in order to appear 'natural'. Further, if gender, sexuality and forms of sexuality such as heterosexuality are simulations and performances, the notion of a fixed, essentialist 'man' or 'woman' is no longer possible.[9] Performativity not identity or essence. Catherine MacKinnon wrote in "Feminism, Marxism, Method, and the State: An Agenda for Theory":

> Sexuality is that social process which creates, organizes, expresses, and directs desire, creating the social beings we know as women and men, as their relations create society.[10]

Adrienne Rich, in her influential essay "Compulsory heterosexuality and lesbian existence", says that heterosexuality is not 'preferred' or chosen, but has to be 'imposed, managed, organized, propagandized, and maintained by force'; in Rich's classic second wave feminist view, 'violent structures' are required by patriarchal society in order to 'enforce women's total emotional, erotic loyalty and subservience to men' (1980).

Thomas Hardy's female protagonists can be seen as characters struggling to attain coherent social and sexual identity, to become an independent body and soul, someone who can exist independently of a patriarchal culture. Critics have noted that figures such as Sue Bridehead in 1895's *Jude the Obscure* are versions of the late Victorian 'New Woman'. Indeed, Sue proposes a number of feminist views, and *Jude the Obscure* is an early feminist work, in which relationships between the sexes and notions of gender are examined in the light of what Thomas Hardy might call 'progressive' philosophy. In *Jude the Obscure,* more than in any of his other works, Hardy grapples with the notion of an emergent 'New Woman', and a heartfelt proto-feminism.[11] At the same time, so-called 'New Woman' fiction was already going out of fashion when *Jude the Obscure* was published (1895); also, the 'New Woman' was not wholly feminist (P. Boumelha, 1982, 136-7).

One can see some of Thomas Hardy's other female protagonists as would-be feminists, as women struggling against patriarchy.[12]

Each, in their own way, is trying to affirm her identity in the face of patriarchy. Tess, Marty South (*The Woodlanders*), Eustacia Vye (*The Return of the Native*), Elizabeth-Jane (*The Mayor of Casterbridge*) and Sue Bridehead (*Jude the Obscure*) question, not always in obvious or outspoken ways, the rigours of patriarchy. Characters such as Tess, Eustacia, Sue and Elizabeth-Jane, in particular, are forms of woman as 'outsider' figures who inhabit what feminists term 'the wild zone'. It's not perhaps surprising that Thomas Hardy should be so close to some aspects of contemporary feminism, in particular the notion of 'woman' as one of the marginalized, dispossessed peoples.

Julia Kristeva and Luce Irigaray, among other French feminists, have spoken of something in 'women' or the 'feminine' that is 'unrepresentable', beyond art, beyond male culture. In *About Chinese Women* (1977), Kristeva writes of the woman as a witch, someone outside of patriarchal discourse, or at least, thrown to the edge, the border between the known zone and the wild zone:

> ...*woman is a specialist in the unconscious, a witch, a bacchanalian, taking her* jouissance *in an anti-Apollonian, Dionysian orgy. A* jouissance *which breaks the symbolic chain, the taboo, the mastery. A* **marginal discourse,** **with regard to the science, religion and philosophy of the** *polis (witch, child, underdeveloped, not even a poet, at best his accomplice).* (*The Kristeva Reader*, 154)

Tess Durbeyfield is called a 'witch' by Alec d'Urberville, but the meaning here is witch = whore (the 'Witch of Babylon'). In 1878's *The Return of the Native*, Eustacia Vye is not only likened to a witch, she is physically attacked by a superstitious local, Susan Nonsuch, who pierces her in church with a needle, echoing the 'pricking' of witches in mediæval times. Sherry Ortner writes that 'woman is being identified with – or, if you will, seems to be a symbol of – something that every culture devalues'.[13] Ann Rosalind Jones describes Julia Kristeva's notion of the 'outsider' culture of women, of women as 'witches':

> *Women, for Kristeva… speak and write as "hysterics," as outsiders to male-dominated discourse, for two reasons: the predominance in them of drives related to anality and childbirth, and their marginal position vis-à-vis masculine culture. Their semiotic style is likely to involve repetitive, spasmodic separations from the dominating discourse, which, more often, they are forced to imitate.*[14]

Julia Kristeva's writings may be the most coherent and incisive account of the psycho-cultural 'wild zone'. For Kristeva, Christianity offers a limited number of ways in which women can participate in the 'symbolic Christian order': for the woman who is not a virgin or a nun (like Thomas Hardy's heroines), who is sexual, has orgasms and gives birth:

> *her only means of gaining access to the symbolic paternal order is by engaging in an endless struggle between the orgasmic maternal body and the symbolic prohibition – a struggle that will take the form of guilt and mortification, and culminates in masochistic* **jouissance.** *For a woman who has not easily repressed her relationship with her mother, participation in the symbolic paternal order as Christianity defines it can only be masochistic.* (1986, 147)

This applies to Thomas Hardy's characters such as Sue Bridehead and Tess. Two of the classic ways in which women have been allowed to participate in Christianity is the *'ecstatic* and the *melancholy'* (ib.). That is, as mystics, or saints, or nuns.

The godfather of the Surrealists André Breton said that 'existence is elsewhere'. French feminists say that 'woman' is elsewhere. 'She is indefinitely other in herself,' comments Luce Irigaray, maintaining that women

> *are already elsewhere than in the discursive machinery where you claim to take them by surprise. They have turned back within themselves, which does not mean the same thing as 'within yourself'. They do not experience the same interiority that you do and which perhaps you mistakenly presume they share.*[15]

Here, perhaps, in the female 'wild zone', some of the wildness and strangeness and ecstasy of 'female' eroticism may be experienced and depicted. For some feminists, Luce Irigaray's morphology of female creativity is empowering,

> a challenge to the traditional construction of feminine morphology where the bodies of women are seen as receptacles for masculine completeness.[16]

Many feminists suggest that women's eroticism cannot be represented, much as women themselves cannot be represented. Julia Kristeva writes in "La femme, ce n'est jamais ça":

> In "woman" I see something that cannot be represented, something that is not said, something above and beyond nomenclatures and ideologies.[17]

Other feminists echo this idea, that women cannot be fully represented in the traditional media of patriarchy. As Hélène Cixous remarked in "Sorties":

> It is at the level of sexual pleasure in my opinion that the difference makes itself most clearly apparent in as far as woman's libidinal economy is neither identifiable by a man nor referable to the masculine economy.[18]

The unrepresentable in art and erotica, according to some feminists, is women's eroticism, their *jouissance*, that 'explosive, blossoming, sane and inexhaustible *jouissance* of the woman', as Julia Kristeva describes it.[19]

Sue and Jude's non-marital state in *Jude the Obscure* disrupts the conventional notions of sexual relationships in late 19th century society. There are even more disruptive erotic relationships possible, though, such as homosexuality and lesbiansim. Even more potentially 'subversive', as far as hetero-patriarchy is concerned, are lesbian motherhood, or sexual representations between cross-dressing, transvestite or transsexual partners. There is no erotic relationship in Thomas Hardy's fiction that approaches such unorthodoxy or 'fucking with gender', and there's only one representation that's seen as 'lesbian' by Hardy critics (Miss Aldclyffe and Cytherea Graye in *Desperate Remedies*). Describing

Miss Aldclyffe's reaction to Cytherea helping her undress, a (male) Hardy critic (Martin Seymour-Smith) says that Miss Aldclyffe's rigid body and firmly closed mouth 'is how a forty-six-year-old sexually excited woman in such a situation would behave' (1995, 129). What a dumb pronouncement.

There are other relationships between women which Thomas Hardy critics, if coaxed, might admit have some lesbian elements: Grace and Felice lost in the woods and clinging to each other in *The Woodlanders*, their dialogue becoming more and more intimate; and Tess and the 'sisterhood' at Talbothays and Marlott in *Tess of the d'Urbervilles*.

> *When women use* je *as the subject of a sentence, this woman* je *most often addresses a man and not another woman or women. It does not relate to itself either*

asserts Luce Irigaray (1994, 46). Gay male eroticism can be discerned in many of the friendships in Thomas Hardy's fiction. This often occurs when lovers of the same woman meet and commune in the socio-sexual trade of women between men that Luce Irigaray identified (Wildeve and Venn in *The Return of the Native*; Oak and Boldwood in *Far From the Madding Crowd*). In Hardy's fiction, only mild forms of 'gender-play', 'gender bending', 'gender-fucking' or 'fucking with gender' occur.[20]

The sexual relations in Thomas Hardy's fiction overwhelmingly conform to the heteropatriarchal model (but that is to be expected to a degree – not least because of the economic, industrial, social and political contexts of magazine publishing in the 1870s-1890s in Great Britain). Anything non-monogamous or adulterous is viewed with horror by some parts of the Wessex community in the novels.

What is surprising, perhaps, is the number of feminists in the early 21st century who also believed in (heterosexual) monogamy as the goal. Even for some radical feminists, lovers still have to be wholly committed to monogamy.[21] Men must not be interested in other women. They are not even allowed to look at pictures of naked women – this is seen as tantamount to adultery. 'I should be everything for him', the devoted wife complains when she finds pornography in her husband's closet. But, Christobel Mackenzie asks in "The Anti-Sexism Campaign Invites You to Fight Sexism, Not Sex", '[w]hat can this possibly have to do with the real relationships people have?'[22] That is, looking at porno is one thing, but does it mean a total breakdown in a relationship? Or looking at other people, perhaps with desire?

Thomas Hardy's fiction explores this heterosexism, which states that heterosexual couplism must be the norm, with the total devotion of each partner to the other. One is not allowed to glance at anyone else, or speak about them (many Hardy characters are jealous). Having no relationship is no good either: the individual is soon hounded by society to conform and marry. Thus, Bathsheba in *Far From the Madding Crowd*, when Troy's buggered off, has the ageing, grim Boldwood on one side waiting patiently but tremulously for her signal to agree to wed him after six years, and Gabriel Oak on the other side, waiting even more patiently, and threatening to leave for California. In *Desperate Remedies* the narrator's bitter comment applies to many of the later Hardy heroines (Grace with Fitzpiers in *The Woodlanders*, Bathsheba with Troy in *Far From the Madding Crowd*, and Tess with Alec in *Tess*):

> *Of all the ingenious and cruel satires that from the beginning till now have been stuck like knives into womankind, surely there is not one so lacerating to them, and to us who love them, as the trite old fact, that the most wretched of men can, in the twinkling of an eye, find a wife ready to be more wretched still for the sake of his company.* (16. 4)

As one critic notes, while for Thomas Hardy's men the crisis may be intellectual or ethical, for Hardy's women it 'is always sexual in nature'.[23]

Language is central to the creation of a 'feminist æsthetics'. Women are denied the place to really *speak*, as many feminists note. Luce Irigaray remarked:

> When a girl begins to talk, she is already unable to speak of/to herself. Being exiled in man's speech, she is already unable to auto-affect. Man's language separates her from her mother and from other women, and she speaks it without speaking in it.24

In *The Woodlanders*, Grace Melbury, like many other Thomas Hardy heroines, does not have men's deftness with language. The narrator says that '[s]he could not explain the subtleties of her feelings as clearly as he [her father] could state his opinion' (XXII). Firm masculine opinion or fact is set against feminine subtlety which verges on the inarticulate. The poet, in a sense, writes inside the mother, or from the mother, or from the maternal realm. 'The poet's *jouissance* that causes him to emerge from schizophrenic decorporealization is the *jouissance* of the mother', remarked Julia Kristeva in *Desire in Language* (1986, 192). But why, Kristeva asks, 'is the speaking subject incapable of uttering the mother within her very self? Why is it that the "mother herself" does not exist?' And why, Kristeva adds, is the mother only phallic? (194).

THOMAS HARDY AND JACQUES LACAN

Biographers and critics of Thomas Hardy have long remarked upon his witnessing of two hangings. The first one occurred on August 9, 1856, when the 16 year-old Hardy saw Martha Brown hanged. The sight apparently deeply impressed Hardy. The erotic component, related in the *Life* – seeing her 'tight black silk gown' accentuating her figure – was also evident, according to Hardy's biographer. 'No boy of sixteen could have escaped being affected by the ghastly juxtaposition of sex and death' (commented Martin Seymour-Smith in his biography [33]). It wasn't just sex and death that were combined, it was sex, death and *looking*. In the *Life* Hardy feels guilty for witnessing the hanging.

The intense scopophilic element was also in evidence in the other execution Thomas Hardy witnessed. While living at Bockhampton, he heard about the hanging taking place in Dorchester at eight in the morning. He went onto the heath with a brass telescope to see it. Just as he put the 'scope to his eye he saw the white figure falling.

> *The whole thing had been so sudden* [he writes in the *Life*], *that the glass nearly fell from Hardy's hands. He seemed alone on the heath with the hanged man, and crept home wishing he had not been so curious.*

It is the last sentence that speaks of the intensity of the experience – he felt alone on the heath with the hanged man, there was a sense of total identification with the victim, with the drama of the execution. After the intensity, comes the guilt at having witnessed the event; Thomas Hardy reacts like people who gleefully watch horror movies then wish afterwards that they hadn't: the images of violence often persist. Somehow, Hardy realizes, by deliberately going out onto the hill to see the execution, he was implicated in it. The sight of it connects him to the victim, the gallows, the executioner, the officials and the crowd watching. Young Tom Hardy becomes a Peeping Tom. The intensity of this event is emphasized by Hardy's visual description of it: the sun behind him shining on the white gaol, with the 'murderer in white fustian' and the officials in dark clothes.

The next step biographers and critics usually make is to connect these experiences of execution to Tess Durbeyfield's, which's witnessed from a distance. Feminist critics have noted, though, that what is specifically *not seen* is Tess's hanging, her body in its final grotesque act. Instead, the flag indicates her death. What is significant about Thomas Hardy and the executions he witnessed were that he *saw* them, and was guiltily fascinated with them. The ideology of the Lacanian gaze is very much at work in these memories related in the *Life*. One sees them not only in Tess's death, but in most of Hardy's work. As Luce Irigaray says, women remind men of their own body, mortality and nature. Susan Griffin wrote 'a woman's body, by inspiring desire in a man, must recall him to his own body'. This is the age-old linking of women with sex and death.

In the œdipal complex, when the father enters the mother-child dyad, a series of displacements occur and the mother becomes the perpetually lost object (J. Kristeva, 1982, 62f). 'Distance from the 'origin' (the maternal)', writes Mary Ann Doane in *The Desire to Desire: The Woman's Film of the 1940's:*

> *is the prerequisite to desire; and insofar as desire is defined as the excess of demand over a need aligned with the maternal figure, the woman is left behind.* (1987, 173)

In her essay on Thomas Hardy's early novels ("Early Hardy Novels and the Fictional Eye"), Judith Wittenberg speaks of the 'voyeuristic moment' in Hardy's fiction, when the

> *seeing subject and the seen object intersect in a diegetic node that both explicitly and implicitly suggests the way in which the world is constituted in and through the scopic drive.* (1983, 151)

One can see how important looking or voyeurism is in Thomas Hardy's fiction, for voyeurism is founded on keeping a spatial distance between subject and object, as Christian Metz noted in "The Imaginary Signifier".[25] Distancing encourages eroticism, because the system of representation – an image of a woman standing in for the real woman – makes the reality less threatening. And, importantly, representations of the erotic object (women) are easier to manipulate to suit one's own ends than 'real' women, as Hardy's male characters know well.[26] Hardy's lovers love from a distance, but when they behold the beloved up close, their desire withers. When the Hardy lover finally unites with the beloved, the former dissatisfaction returns. 'With contact loves dies' (J. Miller, 1970, 176).

For French feminists such as Hélène Cixous, the philosophy of the Lacanian 'lack' is ridiculous. As she writes in her key essay of 1975, "The Laugh of the Medusa": '[w]hat's a desire originating from a lack? A pretty meagre desire.' (E. Marks, 262) And Luce Irigaray and other feminists (Sarah Kofman, Elizabeth Grosz, Michele Montrelay, Mary Ann Doane) have criticized the Freudian-Lacanian emphasis on the phallus as the 'transcendental signifier', as the measure of authentic sexual pleasure.[27] What woman lacks is lack itself, says Montrelay, an inability to create distance and representation (Tess Durbeyfield is denied this).

From Plato to Sigmund Freud and Jacques Lacan, the desire and lack has been central to Western sexual metaphysics: in this negative model, one is doomed to a desire for more and more consumption, which leads to dissatisfaction. The 'lack' or emptiness at the heart of Thomas Hardy's lovers can only momentarily be filled. Erotic plenitude never lasts (J. Miller, 1970, 184). Freudian-Lacanian desire can never be satisfied: dissatisfaction is built-in. Desire is never annihilated: for Georg Wilhelm Friedrich Hegel, only another desire can satisfy desire and also perpetuate it. Desire thus desires more desire (this has a vivid expression in late capitalist consumerism, where it is always the *next* commodity that will truly satisfy and stop the hunger for more objects. But it never happens).

Another way of looking at desire is not to see it as the (unattainable) search for satisfaction stemming from a lack (Jacques Lacan), nor as related to denial and prohibition (Sigmund Freud), but rather as a positive force of fullness and production, that creates interactions, that makes connections between things. Instead of internalization and obliteration (Hegel), desire may join and make things (Friedrich Nietzsche and Benedict Spinoza). For Gilles Deleuze and Félix Guattari (*pace* Spinoza and Nietzsche), desire is a positive force, 'inherently full. Instead of a yearning, desire is seen as an actualization, a series of practices, action, production' (Elizabeth Grosz).[28] As Hélène Cixous says: 'my desires have invented new desires' (E. Marks, 246).

The Lacanian Look emphasizes eroticism. Seeing is erotic, the eye becomes a kind of phallus, caressing the obscure object of desire, which it can never 'possess'. As the poet Rainer Maria Rilke wrote (and Thomas Hardy would concur): '[g]azing is a wonderful thing.'[29] The act of looking eroticizes the object. The Look is an assertion of male power and sexuality. 'Male desire is presented as a response to female beauty', states Andrea Dworkin in *Intercourse* (114).

Lacanian psychoanalysis is a hell of misrepresentations and misreadings, mirrors and imaginary spaces. The subject in the Lacanian system is constantly trying to make good mistakes made in its early psychosexual growth. In the dreaded mirror phase, the image becomes a mirage, and a distance is set up between the image and the body, an absence which Lacan termed the *objet a*. In the confusions of the three realms, the symbolic, real and imaginary, the subject cannot realize what it most wants to realize. The objects of desire remain forever elusive (like Angel Clare longing for Tess Durbeyfield, and vice versa).

There is something inexplicably depressing about Jacques Lacan's version of psychosexual events. Lovers, in the Lacanian system, desire what they cannot have. The problem of the lack, the *objet a* and *la chose*, can never be resolved. Lacanian philosophy posits, among other things (here we go): an eternal search for what can never be found.[30] The Freudian-Lacanian system demands a continuous series of substitutions for the objects to fill the primordial lack. It is a system of replacing an imaginary and immobile plenitude that will always fail. The primal realm remains always lost or forbidden. The paradise of early childhood recedes ever further into the distance of the past.

In the Jungian system, Beatrice, Laura, Cleopatra, Isolde, Eurydice, Ariadne and all those women of myth, poetry and legend, are incarnations of the *anima*, which is, as Carl Jung explained in *The Development of Personality*, something all males possess: '[e]very man carries with him the eternal image of woman, not the image of this or that particular woman, but a definitive feminine image.'[31] The *anima* is 'a personification of the unconscious in a man, which appears as a woman or a goddess in dreams, visions and creative fantasies', write Emma Jung and Marie-Louise von Franz.[32] Male writers throughout history have depicted their version of the *anima*, it seems. Each (male) writer has a version of the 'inner feminine figure', as Carl Jung calls her (1967, 210-1). For artists, this idealized *anima* figure seems to be another manifestation of that obscure object of desire, the eroticized woman, a mirror for male lust. The equation is: the more sublime and voluptuous the woman is depicted, the more sublime and voluptuous is the artist's desire. In Thomas Hardy's fiction, characters such as Sue Bridehead, Tess Durbeyfield and Eustacia Vye have a powerful *anima* component for their male suitors.

Further; in Lacanian psychology, desire, which is the foundation of the system, is enmeshed with speaking, with creativity and art. The œdipal crisis and the repression of the desire for the mother occurs with the entry into the Symbolic Order, and the entry into language. As Toril Moi crystallizes Lacan's thought so concisely in *Sexual/ Textual Politics: Feminist Literary Theory*: '[t]o speak as a subject is therefore the same as to represent the existence of repressed desire.' (1988, 99-100) Men gaze at women and manipulate them into erotic poses (Jude with Sue in *Jude the Obscure*, Alec and Angel with Tess in *Tess of the d'Urbervilles*, Wildeve and Clym with Eustacia in *The Return of the Native*, and Henchard, problematically, with Elizabeth-Jane in *The Mayor of Casterbridge*).

The most intense sequence of erotic looking in Thomas Hardy's fiction occurs in the opening of *Far From the Madding Crowd*. Here is the classic Lacanian scenario of a man looking at a woman without her knowing. The Lacanian/ filmic undercurrent is exaggerated when Bathsheba Everdene takes out a mirror and looks at herself, smiling. The language depicts erotic pleasure – Bathsheba has her eyes half-closed, parts her lips and smiles, and blushes profusely. The narrator even reminds the reader of the novelty of the event taking place outdoors, instead of in a bedroom (chapter I). When Oak confronts Bathsheba, returning her hat, Hardy's narrator makes the power of phallic voyeurism explicit:

> *Rays of male vision seem to have a tickling effect upon virgin faces in rural districts; she brushed hers with her hand as if Gabriel had been irritating its pink surface by actual touch...* (III)

The intensity of Lacanian desire and Freudian projection is underlined at the end of chapter II of *Far From the Madding Crowd* when Gabriel Oak is described as having a lack or void inside him:

> *Having for some time known the want of a satisfactory form to fill an increasing void within him, his position moreover affording the widest scope for his fancy, he painted her a beauty.* (II)

Jude Fawley in Thomas Hardy's last novel has the same lack inside him after seeing Arabella for the first time: before meeting her, he didn't know it was there. Similarly, before Gabriel meets Bathsheba, he is reasonably content. Her arrival makes him realize his life is not complete without a woman.

THOMAS HARDY AND LUCE IRIGARAY

The pleasure of the text, whether the text is a painting, film, magazine, photograph, piece of theatre, and so on, comes, according to Roland Barthes, when the look of the spectator is aligned with that of the author.[33] Judith Wittenberg speaks of Thomas Hardy's 'spectatorial narrator' (1983, 152). What feminist criticism has done is to question the masculine 'pleasure of the text', arguing for a feminist reading of the traditional masculine or patriarchal view of texts. This debate has been central to feminism's approach to Hardy's fiction – the problem of the gender of the narrator and spectator.

> *Hardy's narrators persist in constructing and interpreting female characters according to standard notions about woman's weakness, inconstancy, and tendency to hysteria*

commented Kristin Brady.[34]

For some feminists, there can be no true 'feminist gaze', because the look is always masculine, ultimately. If the spectator is a 'gendered object', suggests Annette Kuhn in *Women's Pictures: Feminism and the Cinema*, then 'masculine subjectivity [is] the only subjectivity available' (1982, 63). The politics of representation, which are central to the consumption of culture and art, are weighted firmly in favour of men and patriarchy. As John Berger writes: 'men act and women appear'. Catherine King notes in "The Politics of Representation: A Democracy of the Gaze":

> *most images in masculine visual ideology are created to empower men as spectators – that is, to see themselves as endlessly important with things laid out for their desire.*[35]

Post-Lacanian feminists such as Luce Irigaray argue that subjectivity can only be attributed to women with difficulty. Irigaray claims that 'any theory of the subject has always been appropriated by the 'masculine'' (in *Speculum of the Other Woman*, 133). 'Woman' is tied to a 'non-subjective subjectum' (ib., 265). Irigaray stresses the sexed being, the sexualized subject and speaking position. No form of knowledge or philosophy can be authentic or 'universal' if it ignores the 'female' position.

Luce Irigaray concentrates on the act of enunciation, the act of producing discourse. Irigaray stresses the interiority of the speaking subject, the traces of subjectivity found in acts of communication. The continual denial of a sexualized discourse threatens the possibility of an emergent non-patriarchal society.

Irigaray has investigated the use by men and women of everyday language, concluding that men and women privilege different patterns of speech, with men encouraging their 'self-affection', or relations to/ with the self and the self projecting in others, while women use language to make connections and relationships with both sexes. Irigaray's deconstruction of the languages of science, philosophy and politics has demonstrated the repression of the feminine – Dale Spender and other feminists have come to similar conclusions. For Irigaray, this repression is not in-built into language, but reflects the (patriarchal) social order. In order to change one the other must also be changed.

Luce Irigaray's argument fits in exactly to a feminist reading of Thomas Hardy's fiction, in particular of *Tess of the d'Urbervilles* as a study of the relations between speaking, language, sexuality, identity, power and patriarchy. Irigaray says that if the vagina is regarded as a 'hole', it is a 'negative' space that cannot be represented in the dominant discourse. Thus to have a vagina is to be deprived of a voice, to be decentred or culturally subordinated, and so Irigaray replaces Lacan's mirror with a vaginal speculum.[36]

One feminist critic of *Tess of the d'Urbervilles* puns Tess Durbeyfield's 'wholeness' with her 'holeness', that is, Tess as sexual lack or vagina waiting to be filled by the male characters and the reader gendered as male by the narration.[37] The phallic privileging of the masculine 'I' (penis, phallus, power, identity, soul – Alec d'Urberville and Angel Clare), means that female sexuality is rendered 'invisible', just as the vulva is a negative space or void (Tess). The phallus is the divine, beloved mirror, emblem of masculine narcissism ('"You are Eve, and I am the old Other One"', mocks Alec in chapter 50).

But the vulva, being a 'black hole', can reflect back nothing. There is no self there. Male speculations and narcissistic gazes create a male subject: the mistakes arise when this male subject is equated with the whole world. This occurs in the perception of Alec d'Urberville and Angel Clare, who cannot comprehend realms of sexuality and ideology outside of the phallocentric, patriarchal norms. The universality of philosophy and psychoanalysis thus becomes founded on a one-sided (male) view of the world (the narrator in Thomas Hardy's novels also ambiguously embodies this view). Male sexuality and narcissism mistakenly becomes the basis for the universal model of sexuality of psychoanalysis. Female sexuality becomes the negative image of male sexuality, if female subjectivity is considered at all (Sue Bridehead and Tess Durbeyfield continually deny their own sexual desires).

Luce Irigaray writes in *Thinking the Difference: For a Peaceful Revolution* that

> *Men always go further, exploit further, seize more, without really knowing where they are going.* (1994, 5)

But it can't be simply a case of 'blaming' men for everything, as Simone de Beauvoir said – blame men, yes, but also blame 'the system' (society). Luce Irigaray thinks that the abstraction 'equality' can only mean *at best* the equality of salaries, so that women will be paid the same as men; nothing else, Irigaray says, can be 'equal'; instead, there must eternal *difference*, in gender, from the sexual to the cultural. Irigaray says that difference must be emphasized, but her theory of difference is based, like the metaphysics of Andrea Dworkin, on sexuality. Sexuality lies at the heart of the feminist discourse of feminists such as Dworkin, Irigaray, Hélène Cixous, Kate Millett, Susan Griffin and Shere Hite; they emphasize sexuality more than other factors, and this is a problem, this reduction, ultimately, to sexual matters. Donna C. Stanton has criticized Cixous' theories, seeing in them a return to the metaphysics of presence and identity, in which the technique of poetic metaphor suggests an economy of similitude, instead of one of difference (1986).

THOMAS HARDY AND LOVE, SEX AND MARRIAGE

Early on in his writing career, at the time of *The Poor Man and the Lady* (1867), when he was 27, Thomas Hardy recognized the importance of erotic desire in fiction:

> as a rule no fiction will considerably interest readers rich or poor unless the passion of love forms a prominent feature in the thread of the story.[64]

Thomas Hardy's characters yearn so painfully – Eustacia Vye in *The Return of the Native* cries out for a great love to help her escape: 'To be loved to madness – such was her great desire' (121). Love – the great yearning – proves to be her downfall. She dies for love, like Cathy in *Wuthering Heights*. Hardy's women yearn, but rarely do they get an earthy lover like Heathcliff. Intense love means intense death. Love now but die later – this is the Romantic credo (and of Shakespearean tragedy). The love between Clym Yeobright and his mother in *The Return of the Native* is equally intense, and destructive. It reaches a profundity of painfulness (VI. i).

Tess Durbeyfield lives, for a season, in 'spiritual altitudes' which are ecstatic (XXXI). Her tragedy is also Eustacia Vye's and Marty South's in *The Woodlanders* – her yearning for love is not reciprocated. Love is not returned, passion burns itself away and is thrust out from the soul into the darkness of the universe. The self is ultimately alone – the modernist post-Romantic stance.

The narrator of *Jude the Obscure* (and also Phillotson) sees Sue and Jude as two halves of one whole – a Gnostic love-union of selves (*Jude*, IV. iv), which's called the *syzygy* in Gnosticism. In fact, their togetherness is very shaky. The dialectic of their love is continually shifting – from desire to disgust, and all the shades in between. There is no easy, simple dualism of reciprocation for Hardy's lovers. Sue and Jude drift apart and come back together in waves. They fuse then fragment, like particles in some sub-atomic experiment. It is a bout of Empodeclean Love and Strife for them, a state of Heraclitean flux, a Hegelian neurotic tension, with the world-weary detachment of Arthur Schopenhauer added.

In Sue and Jude in *Jude the Obscure* the big themes – the pagan and the Christian, the traditional and the modern, the spiritual and the sexual – are at war. Thomas Hardy depicts love-in-flux, always being modulated, changed, destroyed, rebuilt, transfigured. Sue and Jude fly together involuntarily – such as in their kiss on the silent road, when they 'kissed close and long' (IV. iii). But soon they fall apart again. The pattern was laid down long ago in figures of myth such as Isis and Osiris, Ishtar and Tammuz, Anna and Baal, and in the later figures such as Anthony and Cleopatra, Héloïse and Abélard, and Petrarch and Laura. Hardy's narrators are heretical about love. They do not believe in marriage. Their ideas on love have much in common with the mediæval cults and heresies: of courtly love, the Cathars, Templars, Sufism, Albigensian heresy, alchemy and the cults of the Grail and the Black Virgin. Though it is not as strident as in some writers, there is in Hardy's world the urge towards spiritual sublimation, the transcendence of the flesh and the mysticization of the erotic.

Love in Thomas Hardy's world is about two people trying to 'follow their bliss' (Joseph Campbell's term). In Hardy's novels the urge of the lovers is to escape, to find, like Sue and Jude, Angel and Tess, their own niche in the world, away from other, interferring people. Hardy put it utterly plainly and so passionately in his poem 'The Recalcitrants':

Let us off and search, and find a place,
Where yours and mine can be natural lives,
Where no one comes, who dissects and dives
And proclaims that ours is a curious case,
Which its touch of romance can scarcely grace.
(*Complete Poems*, 389)

This is the great dream of lovers – to re-create the world and to find a place in which to really live and breathe. The problem is that society and all kinds of other factors subvert this lust for loneliness. 'Love is the burning-point of life', says Joseph Campbell (*Power*, 205), and the tragedy of Thomas Hardy's novels, as D.H. Lawrence notes in *Study of Thomas Hardy*, is that the pioneers in love die in the wilderness (21).

Escape, but die. Remain, and live.

The Kierkegaardian risk-taking is everything. Without risk there is no life. Life is lived on the edge. This risk-taking for the glory of love is the main theme in Thomas Hardy's fiction. The way he deals with it makes him 'great' – as with Fyodor Dostoievsky or William Shakespeare or Sappho. D.H. Lawrence remarked in *Study of Thomas Hardy*:

> *His feeling, his instinct, his sensuous understanding is, however, apart from his metaphysic, very great and deep, deeper than that perhaps of any other English novelist.* (93)

Thomas Hardy's fiction is full of supernatural sensibilities. He conversed many times with his dead wife, Emma:

> *Would that I lay there*
> *And she were housed here!*
> *Or better, together*
> *Were folded away there*
> *Exposed to one weather*
> *We both…*
>   ('Rain on a Grave', CP, 441)

The Thomas Hardy-poet yearns to be united with his decayed lovers, in the Emily Brontëan manner:

> *The eternal tie which binds us twain in one*
> *No eye will see*
> *Stretching across the miles that sever you from me.* (CP, 421)

The romantic idea of lovers meeting over distances, or at night, in dreams, or after death, extends the Western notion of the soul to its logical extreme. One aim of the writer is to make writing like love – to write and love, to make the act of writing love itself, to make desire concrete in art, the two fusing, love and art, into one life. The aim is to fuse life and love and art. As Hardy wrote in his poetry: '[l]ove lures life on.' ('Lines', in CP, 458).

One of ancient Greek poet Sappho's short lyrics on love reads:

*It brings us pain
and weaves myths.*[65]

This describes concisely the dominant discourse of love in Thomas Hardy's (and most) fiction: the Nietzschean/ Christian emphasis on suffering, and the subsequent myth-making. (Sappho is quoted in *Jude the Obscure*, though with a different meaning – referring to Sue Bridehead in the epigram to 'Part Third, 'At Melchester').

Love in Thomas Hardy's work is Keatsian and Shelleyan. Hardy's work is fleshly, sensuous but also doomed. His love-affairs take much of their flavour from poems such as John Keats' poem 'La Belle Dame Sans Merci'. Elfride, in her vanity, asks Stephen from her pony in *A Pair of Blue Eyes*: '"Do I seem like La belle dame sans merci?"' (57). The reference probably suggested itself to Hardy as he constructed this scene.

*I met a lady in the meads,
    Full beautiful – a faery's child,
Her hair was long, her foot was light,
    And her eyes were wild.*

The fairy queen/ knightly lover motifs feature also in the romances of Bathsheba and Oak in *Far From the Madding Crowd*, Sue and Jude in *Jude the Obscure*, and Eustacia and Clym in *The Return of the Native*. The dark sensualism of John Keats' poetry is well suited to Thomas Hardy's work. Hardy is a slave to love, as a poet, as he is a slave to women, to Woman, like poets such as Dante Alighieri, Francesco Petrarch, John Donne, Robert Herrick and Robert Graves. Hardy's women are Muses who throw down enchantments over the initiate's soul and senses. Hardy's beloveds are the Symbolist and Decadent Fatal Women, the pale wraiths eulogized by poets such as Charles Baudelaire, Algernon Swinburne and Samuel Taylor Coleridge, and by Franz von Stuck, Gustave Moreau and Félicien Rops in painting. Robert Graves had his Laura Riding (an archetypal poet and Muse relation in modern poetry), as Hardy had his Emma Gifford. The poetry records a haunting of the poet-alone by the Elf-Queen.

The literary antecedents of this scenario are many – the classic one in English literature being of course the Shakespeare-poet and his formidable Dark Lady in *The Sonnets*, she '[w]ho art as black as hell, as dark as night' (last line of sonnet no. 147):

> *My love is as a fever longing still,*
> *For that which longer nurseth the disease;*
> *Feeding on that which doth preserve the ill,*
> *The uncertain sickly appetite to please.*
> *My reason, the physician to my love,*
> *Angry that his prescriptions are not kept,*
> *Hath left me, and I desperate now approve*
> *Desire is death, which physic did except.*
> *Past cure I am, now Reason is past care,*
> *And frantic-mad with evermore unrest;*
> *My thoughts and my discourse as madmen's are,*
> *At random from the truth vainly expressed;*
> > *For I have sworn thee fair, and thought thee bright,*
> > *Who art as black as hell, as dark as night.*

Another ancestor is Merlin's enthrallment at the hands of Ninue in Arthurian legend. In the poesie of John Keats, Percy Bysshe Shelley and the Elizabethan poets we find the powerful spirit of Arthuriana, embodied in figures such as the Lady of Shalott or Morgan Le Fey, before they became trivialized in late Victorian poetry and Pre-Raphaelitism. These romantic ideas surged throughout Europe in the late 12th century and afterwards with the troubadours. But England was late in incorporating Arthurian legend. The new concepts and *mœurs* of love and individualism took hold in the Elizabethans. In Thomas Campion's exaltation of the 'fairy queen Prosperina' for instance:

> *Hark all you ladies that do sleep,*
> *The fairy queen Prosperina*
> *Bids you awake, and pity them that weep.*
> *You may do in the dark*
> *What the day doth forbid.*
> *Fear not the dogs that bark;*
> *Night will have all hid.*

Nothing new about these sorcerous Madonnas, however. Giraut de Borneil, Arnaut Daniel, Bernard de Ventadour and the other troubadours, *jongleurs* and minstrels had all done it before, and *so well*, too, in the 11th and 12th centuries.

William Shakespeare is the apotheosis in English literature of this kind of love-poetry. Romanticism is the end of it all – though a wild, chaotic and intense kind of death. Thomas Hardy arrives at the very tail-end of this extended demise. What is raised up in his love-poetry is the authenticity of his experience and poetic voice. Hardy is not as violent, nor as high-flown, as the Elizabethans. Nicholas Breton wrote in *The Passionate Shepherd*: 'to kill love's maladies, | Meet her with your melodies' (in G. Hiller, 244). This is the answer – when stabbed to death by love, re-birth yourself in art, in love-poetry. Or as John Keats would have it in 'Ode To Melancholy':

> *...if thy mistress some rich anger shows*
> *Emprison her soft hand, and let her rave,*
> *And feed deep, deep upon her peerless eyes*

Thomas Hardy's poetic persona is not as assertive as John Keats or William Shakespeare, though there is still the same masochistic misogyny in some of his poetry. The Hardyan lover though, like Shakespeare, wants to be slain by his beloved. 'Kill me outright with looks', implores the Shakespeare-poet, while Jude, at the agonizing climax of his romance with Sue in *Jude the Obscure*, also implores his black Mistress:

"Don't go – don't go!... This is my last time! I... shall never come again. Don't then be unmerciful, Sue, Sue! we are acting by the letter, and the letter killeth!" (Jude the Obscure, VI. viii)

The letter, the vicious law of a dying religion, Christianity, certainly does kill. So the poet begs for *merci*, that key blessing in Renaissance and chivalric love-poetry. But the poet knows it is useless – it is all over, just as Tess Durbeyfield cries, but hopelessly '"Have Mercy!"' (XXXV) The romances of Jude-Sue and Angel-Tess have a Shelleyan subtext to them. They are built upon an ætherealizing orientation of spirit-over-sex. Love without touching, sex through spirituality, a deeply sensuous love-act transcending skin and ordinary sense – this is a common ambition in Hardyan Wessexuality. Think of all those poems of Hardy's, in which the poet meets some beloved by night, but they do not touch or kiss, just talk. Hardy aims to spiritualize love, but in a heterodox, not doctrinal, manner.

Jude the Obscure records the failure of this sacralization of love, its near-impossible fusion with everyday domestic and economic life. Thomas Hardy's holy love, like Percy Bysshe Shelley's, needs a sacred, secret place away from other people, in which to flourish. But there's none left, there's nowhere to go. So one has to create one's own – and how difficult that is. Hardy's lovers aim to do this: '[l]et us off and search, and find a place', Hardy wrote in 'The Recalcitrants'. But they fail. Robert Herrick wrote the same pæan in 'Corrinna's Going-a-Maying': '[c]ome, let us go while we are in our prime'. It is an anti-social ambition, an escapism in love almost wholly unrealizable.

Thomas Hardy is very bitter about this secular failure to recapture an earlier hermetic love-time. In his poem 'She to Him I' he wrote: '[t]hat Sportsman Time but rears his brood to kill' (CP, 15). This is the bleak view of Tess Durbeyfield, who wishes she'd never been born into this cynical game of the gods. Hardy tries to look honestly and clearly at life – to go after the 'offensive truth' (Per, 26). His pessimism is really 'evolutionary meliorism' (ib, 52). As he says in the poem 'In Tenebris': 'if a Better way there be, it exacts a full look at the Worst' (CP, 168). Hardy depicts people full of 'fret and fever' (Per, 42), the idea is: 'given the man and woman, how to find a basis for their sexual relation' (ib, 19). Hardy quotes his beloved William Shakespeare in support of his claims: 'life [is] time's fool' (Per, 47, quoting *King Henry IV* i, V, iv, 81). The flipside is '[l]ove's not Time's fool' (sonnet no. 116).

The work of William Shakespeare and Thomas Hardy is the result of the attempt to fuse these two viewpoints – the hopeless and the idealistic. Love's not time's fool, but life is – how typical of two realist and often determinist artists to be so ambivalent. They know love and life and art and time and death cannot be simply reconciled. In the work of both Hardy and Shakespeare, Time marches on, unstoppable, even though, sometimes, it 'must have a stop'. No. It eats everything away, demolishing all as it sweeps by. Wes-sex-mania ends up as a drowned body in a heathland river (*The Return of the Native*), or a hanged woman in a Winchester goal (*Tess of the d'Urbervilles*), or a derelict dying in Oxford (*Jude the Obscure*), or a corpse in a Dorset wood (*The Woodlanders*).

How desolate Thomas Hardy's view of the outcome of love seems to be. He is an optimist blasted by life's shocks into bitter realism. His works record satires of circumstance, life's little ironies and time's laughingstocks, those human shows with their few moments of vision, offensive truths hidden amongst post-pastoral Wessex tales.

How forlorn Thomas Hardy actually is can be adjudged from the endings to his tragic novels, and throughout his poetry. Tragedies must end in death, it seems (but how awful and ludicrous is Viviette's collapse at the end of *Two on a Tower*). There is much doom and gloom in the poetry. It is there in the early poems – in 'Neutral Tones', for example. Hardy's imagery in this short lyric is bleak, while the poem's sparseness looks forward to Samuel Beckett: the white sun, dead pond, barren earth (these are stage-settings for *Waiting For Godot* or *Happy Days*). Hardy rages here, too, though in a quiet way – the poet learns that 'love deceives' and thus the sun, the innocent, utterly non-human sun, becomes 'God-curst' (CP, 12). This is typical of the love-poem in the West: the jilted lover must have the outside world reflect his/her desolation.

The futile scene in 'Neutral Tones' is picked up in Thomas Hardy's last novel – it forms the opening of *Jude the Obscure*. Jude, the 'natural boy', works in the 'wide and lonely depression of the empty field' (I. iii). The depth of Hardy's rage is clear from the way he develops this scene – Jude soon gets beaten up by Farmer Troughton, and whirled around like a toy. The target of Hardy's anger is made explicit – it is not God, nor the birds nor nature, but the human world in which Jude lives (I. iii).

Thomas Hardy is bitterly ironic in his use of Percy Bysshe Shelley as one of the major discourses in *Jude the Obscure*. Hardy counters his grim realism with a Shelleyan aching for sweetness and release. It is this quivering yearning that powers Eustacia Vye, Tess Durbeyfield, Sue Bridehead and Jude Fawley, and also Jocelyn Pierston in *The Well-Beloved* in his Platonic search for a Shelleyan 'Beloved'. Eustacia, Tess and Sue are Shelleyan heroines, yearning for a delicacy of touch and spirit that the workaday world simply cannot provide. The gulfs between the two form the tension at the heart of the Hardy novel (*Life*, 272). These conflicts force the Hardyan anti-hero to cry, with Shelley: 'O World, o Life, o Time'.

Thomas Hardy can be seen as ultimately an optimist. He does weave in an escape-clause at the end of his novels, most prophetically (and ambiguously) in the figures of Angel and Tess's sister, as a New Adam and Eve. And in 'The Darkling Thrush', with its heartfelt synthesis of the poetry of John Keats, Percy Shelley and William Wordsworth, Hardy rejoices that out of the waste land a bird can still sing, and that

there trembled through
His happy good-night air
Some blessed Hope (CP, 150)

The Promethean rebellion in Thomas Hardy's fiction occurs in sexual politics and erotic desire. For Hardy's disaffected, dispossessed, depressed and often displaced characters, the way out is through/ by / in/ with love. In Hardy's fictive world, religion no longer offers moments of ecstasy and union, but love, the 'profane' experience, still does. What Jude Fawley does is what all Hardy's lovers do: he creates a religion of love around Sue Bridehead, what Stendhal called the 'crystallization of love'.[40]

The problems arise because there is a gulf between the individual's wishes and what society demands of the individual. What Jude does in *Jude the Obscure* is to build up a cult or religious aura around Sue, and the more it's built up, the greater his fall will be. Aunt Druisilla recognizes the danger of such erotic objectification and warns Jude against it. Jude has to realize, and it's painful, that Sue will not conform to his psychic projection of her as a virginal essence. In the Godless world of Hardy's lovers, the beloved has to stand in for divinity, much as the lady of courtly love poetry was a divinity akin to the Virgin Mary. However, no individual can replace God or divinity, and the result is always disillusion for Hardy's lovers.

The American Jungian Joseph Campbell wrote of marriage:

> *There are two stages* [of marriage]. *First is what I call the biological stage which has to do with producing and raising children, and the other is what I would the alchemical marriage – realizing the spiritual identity that the two are somehow one person. It is the image of the androgyne, the male/ female being. That is the image of what is being realized through a marriage. In that mythological reference the two are one. (This business, 22)*

Thomas Hardy's couples rarely even get to the physical/ sexual/ parental stage, let alone the spiritual/ alchemical stage. Often they are in a rush to be spiritually fused, and ignore everything else. They trip up. The sexual/ domestic level is so problematic that the spiritual/ emotional side has no hope of working out successfully. In Hardy's world of love, the two-in-oneness is continually scuppered by the demands of sexuality, materialism, economics, politics and society. In Hardy's fiction, 'weddings be funerals', as Widow Edlin put it in *Jude the Obscure*. Marriage is called wed*lock*. Arabella brandishes the 'padlock' of wedlock (her wedding ring) to her neighbours in her second marriage with Jude.

It's usual for tragedies to end with death, while romances, fairy tales and comedies climax with marriage. In Thomas Hardy's fiction, tragedies often begin with marriage, while the 'pastoral' or 'romance' novels always contain marriage. Interestingly, Hardy described Tess's condition in the latter part of the narrative as being a living death: for Hardy, Tess Durbeyfield is a 'mere corpse drifting with a current to her end' (E. Blunden, 1942). A curious way to regard one's favourite heroine, but typically Hardyan.

The alchemical 'two-in-oneness' is most powerfully evoked in *Jude the Obscure*, but it occurs throughout Thomas Hardy's work, as throughout Western culture. There is always the hope that, somewhere, somehow, at some time, a sexual love can be united with a spiritual love. It is this desire for a unity of sex and spirit as well as two lovers, that lies behind *Romeo and Juliet*, Dante Alighieri's *Vita Nuova*, Francesco Petrarch's *Canzoniere*, John Donne's *Songs and Sonnets* and Emily Brontë's *Wuthering Heights*. Hardy's lovers believe, against all the odds, in the spiritualization of love. They know the sexualization of love, this is what provides the stories with much of their dramatic tension. Love exists in a nostalgic past or in a never-to-be-attained future. 'The *meeting*, then, mixing pleasure and promise or hopes, remains in a sort of future perfect', writes Julia Kristeva.[41]

The relation between love and language for Kristeva pivots around primary narcissism:

> ...when one transposes into language the idealization on the edge of primal repression that amatory experience amounts to, this assumes that scription and writer invest in language in the first place precisely because it is a favourite object – a place for excess and absurdity, ecstasy and death. Putt-

ing love into words... necessarily summons up not the narcissistic parry *but what appears to me as narcissistic* economy. *(Tales of Love,* 267-8)

Writing of love perpetuates the 'narcissistic economy'. To explore her psychoanalytic theory of love, Julia Kristeva often employs the tactic of setting things against each other, of opposites. Thus, she explores the realm of the obverse of love – hate. This is another reason, perhaps, why Thomas Hardy turned from novels to poetry, because poetry may be closer to his idea of turning writing into love. Making writing *of* the (love) experience the experience itself.

This idea has a correspondence with the French feminists, with Hélène Cixous and Luce Irigaray, who evoke the *jouissance* of writing, of the sexuality of the text. Cixous speaks of literary texts which deal with 'libidinal education' in "Extreme Fidelity". Cixous' description of these works corresponds to Thomas Hardy's *Tess of the d'Urbervilles, Jude the Obscure, The Return of the Native, The Mayor of Casterbridge* and many others:

> *We have worked on a group of texts which belong to what can be called the literature of apprenticeship, the* Bildungsroman, *and all of the texts – and there are a lot of them because literature is after all their domain – which relate the development of an individual, their story, the story of their soul, the story of their discovery of the world, of its joys and its prohibitions, its joys and its laws, always on the trail of the first story of all human stories, the story of* Eve and the Apple. *World literature abounds in texts of libidinal education, because every writer, every artist, is brought at one moment or another to work on the genesis of his/her own artistic being. It is the supreme text, the one written through a turning back to the place where one plays to win or lose life.*[42]

On one level, artistic creation counters Lacanian lack and Kristevan absence: the act of writing staves off emptiness and loneliness by filling up the psychic space. As Julia Kristeva wrote in "Freud and Love: Treatment and Its Discontents":

> *If narcissism is a defence against the emptiness of separation, then the whole contrivance of imagery, representations, identifications and project-*

ions that accompany it on the way towards strengthening the Ego and the Subject is a means of exorcising that emptiness. (1987, 42)

At the same time, the author's characters can provide much amusement, even a kind of spiritual solace. But the beloved other always remains a mystery. The trouble is, in getting close to another person, all manner of social and psychological problems arise. Or as Hélène Cixous puts it: '[t]here is an apple, and straight away there is the law.' (1994, 133) With the apple comes the law: Eve (woman) is punished, Cixous says, because she has access to the inside, to pleasure, to touching. Eve

> *is punished since she has access to pleasure, of course a positive relationship to the inside is something which threatens society and which must be controlled. That is where the series of "you-shall-not-enter" begins.* (1994, 134)

In *Jude the Obscure* it is 'woman's nature' which 'breaks' up Sue Bridehead and the Sue-Jude relationship – Jude is not ruined by 'man's nature' because 'man's nature' is 'a term and concept that had no currency in the nineteenth century.'[43]

Thomas Hardy's novels so graphically explore the desire and the prohibition, the lust for life and the laws that come down like walls of steel around the soul.[44] One sees this agony of desire and fear so clearly in books such as *Jude the Obscure* and *The Mayor of Casterbridge*, where the apple of temptation is dangled before the protagonists, then the problems begin. At the end of *Two on a Tower* the apple of life is brutally torn away from Swithin's grasp as Viviette dies in his arms (unconvincingly). So close, yet so far away: so much presence, and yet the agony of absence. Hélène Cixous writes:

> *It is the struggle between presence and absence, between an undesirable, unverifiable, indecisive absence, and a presence, a presence which is not only a presence: the apple is visible and it can be held up to the mouth, it is full, it has an* inside. (ib., 133)

Tess Durbeyfield is of course the character in the world of Thomas Hardy most obviously likened to the Biblical Eve. And Tess finds out that the punishment is brutal for those who eat the apple. As soon as the apple appears, the prohibitions appear, the long list of 'thou shalt nots', as Sue Bridehead bitterly knows. Pleasure, in Hardy's world, as in the Christian West, is punished.

"Domestic laws should be made according to temperaments, which should be classified. If people are at all peculiar in character they have to suffer from the very rules that produce comfort in others!"' (233)

Thomas Hardy's lovers won't have anybody else except The One in their sights. All their desire is aimed at one person, and an alternative person won't do. For Jude Fawley it must be Sue Bridehead (in *Jude the Obscure*), for Tess Durbeyfield it must be Angel Clare (in *Tess of the d'Urbervilles*), for Marty South it must be Giles Winterbourne (in *The Woodlanders*), and so on. As American filmmaker Bette Gordon observed, '[u]sually the object of your obsession is less important than the fact of being obsessed.' It's the obsession that counts.[45] If there were a magic formula or potion to make someone love you, the Hardyan lover would do anything to buy it. In fact, Vibert the quack doctor in *Jude the Obscure* does sell a love potion, but it is not of course the Grail.

Thomas Hardy's lovers live on the edge. They are artists of desperation. Desire in Hardy's fiction creates dishonesty: the greater the desire, the more willing the protagonist is to achieve their desire. As John Kucich puts it in "Moral Authority in the Late Novel: The Gendering of Art", 'dishonesty is simply one of the desperate remedies of desire'.[46] The deeper the desire, the greater the risks, and potential rewards. Characters in love become increasingly desperate. Desire entraps the protagonist (often they don't recognize their entrapment), and also produces a desire to entrap other people, especially other lovers.

In *The Woodlanders* Edred Fitzpiers tells Giles Winterbourne, concerning Grace Melbury, that he is in love with '"something in my own head, and no thing-in-itself outside it at all"' (XVI). In Jungian terms, Hardy's male characters have to learn how to integrate the 'feminine' side of themselves, how to discern between the *anima* and the projection of their desires and needs onto other people. Hardy's male protagonists have to assimilate the feminine, a process which is problematical and painful. Henchard, Angel, Jude and Giles find it a real struggle to identify with and assimilate the feminine. Joseph Campbell writes in *This Business of the Gods*:

> *The problem of therapy is to bring the "head" into harmony with the energies that are informing the body, so the transcendent energies can come though. Only when this occurs are you transparent to transcendence. This implies yielding yourself to nature; putting yourself in accord with nature and, I would say, that is the main aim of most of the mythologies of the world.* (25)

This is another way of putting the basic problem in Thomas Hardy's novels, which D.H. Lawrence called the problem of 'coming into being'. Hardy's people are not 'transparent to transcendence', rather, they are earthbound, and continually concentrate on a symbol instead of seeing through it. They are supremely literal. Like children, they have to have results *now*, and physically in front of them. Think of Grace and Giles in *The Woodlanders*, or Sue and Jude in *Jude the Obscure*, or Tess and Angel in *Tess of the d'Urbervilles*, how childish they are, how they cling onto a literal interpretation of events. Hardy's lovers mistake the symbol for the thing itself. Desperate, Hardy's lovers grasp at any sign and analyze it, turning it into something much more than it is. Eustacia Vye, stuck on Egdon Heath in *The Return of the Native*, grasps at anything that might enable her to escape. Hardy's lovers do not recognize the metaphoric aspect of spiritual love. For them, love must have a physical, literal, conscious manifestation. Critics do the same: they read Hardy's fiction literally, seeing in his novels a series of literal events.

The problem of being transparent or opaque to transcendence is at its most acute in *Jude the Obscure,* where the lovers fight to have their kind of supra-sexual, proto-spiritual love accepted by society. They fail, partly because society (in this case the neighbours in Oxford/ Christminster) cannot see that love between a man and woman who appear to be married does not have to be sexual. It is the very appearance of a non-sexual bond, one that, further, has not been sanctified by society and law and the church, that incenses Sue and Jude's neighbours. William Greenslade suggests in *Degeneration, Culture and the Novel 1880-1940* that Sue and Jude could refute biological determinism and

> make their own sexuality the medium of self-definition: the text might then utter what it suppresses but continually intimates. (181)

Sue and Jude try to explore an area where heterosexuality, let alone sexuality, is not 'compulsory'. As feminists have noted, not only is heterosexuality socially and ideologically 'compulsory', in Adrienne Rich's phrase, but sexuality is compulsory: everyone is expected to be sexual, to be sexually active.[47] 'Women are expected to be in, or to want to be in, a sexual relationship'.[48] You see this so clearly with Tess Durbeyfield: Tess's mother is but the first of many people who expects Tess to desire a sexual relationship. Witness Alec's astonishment when she rejects him: *what?* he implies, *you don't desire me?* But not just women: everyone is expected to be sexual.

In the radical (second wave) feminist terminology of Andrea Dworkin, Susan Griffin, Kate Millett and others, being 'sexual' is equated with being possessed sexually. In the patriarchal system, in the view of some feminists, women cannot win: they are condemned if they don't want or have sex, but women who express their sexuality are regarded with suspicion. As adolescents, what is seen as 'natural' for boys to express, sexually, is criminal for girls. Women who admit to liking sex are somehow seen as 'dirty' or 'bad'; this happens to Thomas Hardy's female characters:

> We are so afraid to be seen as 'whores' that we accept the idea of ourselves as 'victims' if we have sex. All this does for women is make being a victim seem natural,

remarked Becky Rosa in "Anti-monogamy: A Radical Challenge to Compulsory Heterosexuality?".[49] Alec d'Urberville calls Tess Durbeyfield a whore in order to justify his seduction of her. Being seen as a 'victim' limits women, and may render them 'inert by self-pity'.[50] Being a prostitute may be the only way in which women are allowed to express themselves sexually in a fiercely patriarchal society. Thus, Alec calls Tess a whore to align himself with patriarchal culture. Christianity divides women into two basic sexual types: the Virgin Mary, the saintly, worshipped Mother, or Mary Magdalene, the whore. Tess may be seen as a latter-day form of the ancient 'holy whore', the sacred prostitutes who served Goddesses such as Cybele and Isis. What's clear is that Tess is not allowed to be both, mother and sexually active woman.

No one, in life or art, it seems, can escape from being defined by their sexual identity and activity. Thus, everyone is branded socially by what they do sexually: so, old people are defined by their sexual *in*activity and jokes are made about the non-performance of their genitals. In the media, in magazines and TV programmes, in films and radio shows, people are depicted either in or not in a sexual relationship, and the sexual relationship takes precedence over all others, over friendship, over being a child or a parent, over business and social relationships. Everyone is expected to be in, or to want to be in, a sexual relationship, and when someone isn't interested, the media hounds them, by making fun of them, by lampooning the individual's non-sexual status.

One sees this social dynamic so clearly in Thomas Hardy's fiction, which is all about the struggle to solve, as he puts it in *The Woodlanders*, 'the immortal puzzle – given the man and woman, how to find a basis for their sexual relation' (39). Hardy said that he felt 'very strongly that the position of man and woman in nature may be taken up and treated frankly' (E. Blunden, 1942).

Thomas Hardy is as obsessed with sex as any other novelist, but that's partly because his texts reflect his socio-cultural environment; because the Western world, from the Renaissance onwards (some would say from Classic Greek times onwards, or earlier), is obsessed with sexuality. Sex is the norm; anything outside of that is regarded suspiciously. Sue and Jude, and Tess, Grace and Anne Garland, are pursued for being non-sexual exactly as modern-day celebrities who don't seem particularly interested in rutting away are regarded as abnormal by the media. It's the time when questions such as this are asked: *what, you haven't got a lover/ car/ house/ cell phone/ I-Pod/ computer/ Blu-ray [insert item as applicable]?* Hardy exposes how society polices itself, how it constructs its sexual norms. Hardy would undoubtedly have ventured into gay and lesbian politics, had he been writing in the 21st century (one wonders how much Hardy would have been sympathetic to, for instance, lesbian feminism, with its talk of femme tops, butch bottoms, femmes butched out, cross-dressing, butch fags in drag, butches 'femmed-out in drag', dildoes, lesbian porn, S/M porn, transvetism, camp and gender-fucking).[51]

The non-sexual activity of the modern celebrity arouses suspicion then often vindictive hassling: the tabloid press ask is s/he gay? perverted? impotent? and so on. As for the idea of friendship, holding hands, dancing, sleeping together, being together, all of this means a sexual relationship is going on: in the media and society, holding hands or walking next to someone or doing the things that romantic, sexual couples do is not allowed unless one *is* a romantic, sexual couple.[52] In Thomas Hardy's novels, if two people hold hands, it is assumed they are in a sexual relationship. Time after time characters hold hands without being in a sexual relationship, then someone sees them. They colour up, they blush, they realize that their every gesture displays to the world their sexual identity. Sometimes it seems that to be sexual at all can be seen as a subversive act, especially outside the 'nuclear family', as American filmmaker Karin Kay noted.[53]

Thomas Hardy's women often faint, collapse, blush, go into a fever, all because of love. So important is love to Hardy's characters, that when love's course goes awry, his characters (especially the women) faint, weep or wither away. They literally die for love. Feelings become expressed physically: their bodies become the biological manifestations of emotions and thoughts. And women, being the 'weaker sex', show more signs of decay than men. Hardy's narrators set out to challenge the norms of gender identity, where women are the 'weaker vessel', lapsing into hysteria, but end up submitting to the patriarchal codes.[54] Unable to describe the response to love internally, Hardy's narrators resort, in women, to extraordinary blushes, palpitations, shiverings, sobs and falls.

It is one of the most annoying aspects of Thomas Hardy's fiction, these sudden blushes or collapses. For example, when Owen recognizes Anne Seaway to be an impostor in *Desperate Remedies*, she colours up like a rainbow: her skin goes ashen grey while her pink cheeks turn purple (18, 1). The insistence on lovers reacting instantly and physically to situations is ridiculous. It is a failure of Hardy's narrators that they can't get inside the characters, but have to show their suffering on the outside (and it's laziness and a lack of imagination on the part of the author). Hardy's women are like painters' canvases or movie screens in this respect, instantly displaying their emotions via uncontrollable tremblings and blushings.

Nature – sexuality, rather – is cruel in Thomas Hardy's fiction. It bypasses delicate education and civilization and careful make-up jobs, erupting in (women's) bodies uncontrollably, showing how they feel, though they might prefer to hide their emotions. Some of Hardy's women react violently to emotional shocks, as if they can't handle them: Viviette shrieks and dies in Swithin's arms in *Two on a Tower*; Miss Aldclyffe bursts a blood vessel and dies after her son's suicide in *Desperate Remedies*; Cytherea, like

Grace, falls ill when it's uncertain about her marital status in *Desperate Remedies*, and so on. (True, some of the women are neurotic, excitable types, but many are earthy, strong, working class women, like Tess Durbeyfield: she's simply too sturdy and tough to faint away).

❦

Underpinning part of *Jude the Obscure* is a utopian vision of a new relation between the sexes. Even the relatively staid Phillotson suggests that single parenthood may be preferable to the traditional nuclear family: '"I don't see why the woman and the children should not be the unit without the man"'. Gillingham responds: '"[b]y the Lord Harry! – Matriarchy!"' (IV. iv). In their lives Sue and Jude are groping towards such a state, although Sue defers to Jude many times, as when she indulges him in his Christminster dream at the Remembrance Day celebrations, even when she knows how destructive it could be. Thomas Hardy's text does not go as far as feminist separatism, though, which some feminists, often lesbian feminists, see as 'the centre, the beating heart, the essence'.[55] In lesbian and radical feminist separatism, women keep themselves not only physically but culturally and psychologically apart from men.[56]

Thomas Hardy did not go as far as advocating such an all-female or matriarchal zone, but one can see how sympathetic Hardy was to feminism, and how he would probably embrace if not radical lesbian separatism, then at least the feminist emphasis on *différance* (*pace* Jacques Derrida, Luce Irigaray and Monique Wittig). The search of Sue and Jude for a cultural place where they can love according to rules they have written themselves chimes with the quest in radical lesbianism for an extra-patriarchal or non-patriarchal space. Much of *Jude the Obscure* is about being 'different' – not biologically or sexually, but socially and culturally. Monique Wittig says that the lesbian is crucial because '[l]esbian is the only concept that I know of which is beyond the categories of sex (man and woman)'.[57]

Thomas Hardy would probably feel sympathetic to the lesbian

and feminist quests for a new kind of socio-sexual identity. The difference is that Hardy posits his opposing discourses (Sue and Jude versus society) wholly within patriarchal culture, while radical lesbian feminism aims to go beyond patriarchy. The lesbian may exist outside of traditional heterosexual discourse, but Sue and Jude do not step beyond it. Sue and Jude are locked into two-term masculine logic, where only 'man' or 'woman' exist. All the characters in *Jude the Obscure* adhere to patriarchal constructions, from Gillingham and Phillotson, to Widow Edlin, Arabella, the people of Christminster and the colleges.

The terrible truth for lovers to learn in Thomas Hardy's fiction is that what one loves most can destroy one. The deeper they sink into love, the worse it gets for Hardy's lovers. Yet even when they are treated appallingly by their beloveds, Hardy's lovers love them even more. They 'desperately apotheosise those who reject their love',[58] they dig their own emotional graves, they hurt even more and wallow in it. Hardy's lovers embrace their own destruction. All Hardy's lovers dream of a total, all-consuming, and lasting love between two adults. This is part of the sovereignty of 'compulsory heterosexuality', as Adrienne Rich calls it. In her essay on *Romeo and Juliet*, Julia Kristeva writes:

If desire is fickle, thirsting for novelty, unstable by definition, what is it that leads love to dream of an eternal couple? Why faithfulness, the wish for a durable harmony, why in short a marriage of love – not as necessity in a given society but as desire, as libidinal necessity?[39]

The problem is that love and the couple is always a problem, is always fraught with problems. Maybe it's because, as Sigmund Freud suggests in "Drives and their vicissitudes", in the narcissism of love, hatred is deeper and more ancient than love.[60] Certainly in Thomas Hardy's fiction, as in most fiction and art, bourgeois romantic love is presented as a struggle, where the lovers are in conflict with the social order (*Jude the Obscure*), with parents and the past (*Tess of the d'Urbervilles*), with neighbours

(*The Return of the Native*), with education and background (*The Woodlanders*), and so on. As Cytherea says in *Desperate Remedies*, '"it is difficult to adjust our outer and inner life with perfect harmony to all!"' (13.3). 'As soon as an *other* appears different from myself, it becomes alien, repelled, repugnant, abject – hated', remarked Julia Kristeva (1987, 22, also 1982).

In Thomas Hardy's novels one sees so clearly the simultaneous desire and revulsion – in the love affair of Sue and Jude, for instance, where the œdipal tension is in conflict with the erotic interplay of lovers.

Thomas Hardy's notion of love, as expressed in his fiction, is so firmly bound up with notions of art and artifice that one cannot discuss love in Hardy's work without mentioning how it is represented in art. For Hardy, the two modes of experience and ideology, love and art, are inseparable. In Hardy's concept of love, the myth of Narcissus is prominent: that is, the self-reflexivity of love, the *mise-en-âbyme* of love, the auto-eroticism of love, love as a crystallizing mirror in the Stendhalian manner.

In Plato's *Symposium*, love is of/ for the other, the other half of one's being. One searches for the completeness to be found in the beloved. The beloved thus becomes that missing fragment which rounds out the desiring self. In Neoplatonism, which develops Plato's philosophy, there is a shift towards a different kind of narcissism. In Plotinus' *Enneads*, love is God, but God is also Narcissus. In Plotinus, the One is 'simultaneously the *loved one* and *love*; He is *love of himself*; for He is beautiful only by and in Himself.' (*Enneads*, VI, 8, 15) With Neoplatonism, a new kind of love is born, one founded on interiority and auto-eroticism. Narcissus loves himself, he is both subject and object. His real object of desire is an image of himself, that is, representation – art.

The appearance of the lover, especially in late adolescence, can be very disruptive, as Tess Durbeyfield, Jude Fawley, Eustacia Vye and Hardy's other doomed lovers find out. In "Narcissus: The New Insanity", Julia Kristeva offers remarks which apply to the fundamental sense of solitude at the heart of Hardy's fiction – that, after love has been enjoyed, and pain is to be endured, solitude is inevitable:

> *Erotic fantasy merges with philosophical meditation in order to reach the focus where the sublime and the abject, making up the pedestal of love, come together in the "flash." ...The contemporary narrative (from Joyce to Bataille) has a posttheological aim: to communicate the amorous flash. The one in which the "I" reaches the paranoid dimensions of the sublime divinity while remaining close to abject collapse, disgust with the self. Or, quite simply, to its moderate version know as solitude.*[61]

If art comes out of the 'crises of subjectivity',[62] as Julia Kristeva suggests (in "Bataille and the Sun, or the Guilty Text") – and any number of artists' work could be cited to support her theory – then melancholy and solitude are inevitable. Melancholy is indeed the natural state of many poets and writers – especially love poets (think of Francesco Petrarch, Bernard de Ventadour, Emily Brontë, Emily Dickinson, William Shakespeare, Louise Labé, and others). The artist writes of love to bring back love. Metaphor becomes the mechanism by which love is reactivated, metaphor becomes 'the point at which ideal and affect come together in language'.[63] So important is writing and making art for some artists, that they are not really 'alive' unless they are making art. Many is the writer who does not feel a day has been spent well unless it has involved some writing. Writers often speak of feeling uneasy (or guilty) if they have not been writing.

Julia Kristeva's description of Fyodor Dostoievsky, in her 1987 study of melancholia, *Black Sun: Depression and Melancholy*, has some bearing on Thomas Hardy's fiction. Dostoievsky, Kristeva asserts, made suffering the keynote of his novels. But it was the 'non-eroticized suffering' of 'primary masochism', that is, melancholy. For Kristeva, Dostoievskian melancholia was 'the primordial psychic inscription of a rupture' (*Black Sun*, 186). Dostoievsky's form of suffering is 'neither inside nor outside, between two, at the threshold of the separation self/ other, even before this is possible' (ib.). In Dostoievsky's fictional world, which has many affinities with Hardy's fictive world, suffering, voluptuously, is essential; humanity is driven by pain, not pleasure.

Thus far, Julia Kristeva's analysis of Fyodor Dostoeivsky relates directly to Thomas Hardy's art. But Kristeva goes further, suggesting that for Dostoeivsky writing produces forgiveness. Dostoeivsky, like Hardy, identified deeply with his characters (like all writers do). Dostoeivsky thus 'travelled hell' with his characters (James Joyce's phrase), just as Hardy does with Tess or Jude or Henchard. The rebirth of the characters becomes the author's own. Writing is thus an act of signifying suffering which produces forgiveness, or as Kristeva has it in *Black Sun*, 'between suffering and acting out, æsthetic activity is forgiveness' (200).

One can see how the relations between forgiveness, suffering and writing relate directly to Thomas Hardy's work. But asking forgiveness of whom? The mother, of course. It is the mother, or a mother-substitute, that the writer asks forgiveness of, according to Julia Kristeva. The mother is the one 'who has been killed by signs in the quest for individuality'. Forgiveness, then, is fundamentally equivalent to a reconciliation with the mother. This also fits in with with the view of Hardy as a writer soaked in the mother-world, in the poetic evocation of (lost) maternal spaces.

3

'Lie or die': Tess of the d'Urbervilles

If there were civil rights for women, the whole of society would be the injured party in the case of rape or all the other forms of violence inflicted on women...

Luce Irigaray, *Je, tu, nous* (88)

Tess of the d'Urbervilles (1891) is a novel of anger, a text which rages against time, God, industrialization, and social institutions such as marriage, Christianity, the Church, law and education. What does Tess Durbeyfield do that is 'wrong'? Thomas Hardy explains in the book: '[s]he had been made to break an accepted social law, but no law known to the environment in which she fancied herself such an anomaly.' (XIII) Tess is forced, or is led, or falls into a complex situation by circumstances, confusions, innocence (or ignorance), bad communication and desire. She is 'made' to break 'an accepted social law': it is the same with

Eustacia Vye, or Sue Bridehead. Somehow, their very existence means transgressions will occur. Tess transgresses society, goes against the grain. She (unwittingly perhaps) places herself outside of society and the law. She learns that there are different kinds of laws – different sets of laws for different groups of people. She has to learn about social boundaries, and how to keep inside of limits. The 'law', or the 'legal system', does not protect Tess from people like Alec d'Urberville, or from being raped. The law does not right the wrong that has been done to Tess, nor does it punish Alec.

As it's a dramatic novel, Tess Durbeyfield learns the hard way. She is seen to be transgressive. The education system fails her utterly, and her mother and family also fail to protect her. Though she is proud of her education, it doesn't help, in the end. A note in *The Life of Thomas Hardy* is usually cited in relation to *Tess of the d'Urbervilles*:

> *When a married woman who has a lover kills her husband, she does not really wish to kill her husband; she wishes to kill the situation.* (289)

The tragedy of *Tess of the d'Urbervilles* has been seen, for example, as:
• the decline of the rural order (John Alcorn, Roger Ebbatson, Merryn Williams);
• the result of commercial forces, in the Marxist model (Raymond Williams);
• a socio-economic destruction (Arnold Kettle);
• the waste of human potential (Irving Howe);
• due to the sexual manipulation of two men (feminist critics such as Penny Boumelha, Kate Millett and Rosalind Sumner);
• due to the heroine's own moral inadequacies (Roy Morrell);
• or as the breaking of social taboos (J. Lecercle), and so on.

In *Tess of the d'Urbervilles* Thomas Hardy's proto-feminism includes a more thorough-going investigation of the male double standard than he had previously undertaken; the exploration of the relationship between sexuality and economy; the questioning of institutions such as the family, marriage, the church, education and class. In *Tess of the d'Urbervilles*, for example, motherhood does not wholly satisfy the heroine: her 'destiny' is not determined by being a mother, though patriarchy might wish to have it so.

Tess of the d'Urbervilles, structurally, is based upon classic oppositions: male-female, active-passive, aristocracy-peasants, present-past, Christianity-paganism, culture-nature, leisure-work, and city-village ('Durbey<u>field</u>' contrasted with 'd'Urber<u>ville</u>'). Hélène Cixous had described such binary logic in her *The Newly Born Woman*. Thomas Hardy simply takes the drama of oppositions and makes them manifest. Thus, Tess Durbeyfield is seen against the steam train, opposing the world of peasants, rural life and femininity with the world of industry, cities, masculinity.

Tess of the d'Urbervilles was produced for the magazine *Graphic*, in weekly instalments in 1891. The novel underwent a number of changes, from its appearance in *Graphic*, to the 'episodic sketches' in *Fortnightly Review* and the *National Observer*, to the editions of 1891, 1892, 1895, 1902 and 1912 (J. Laird, 1975, v). At the stage of the one-volume edition of *Tess*, Thomas Hardy was still changing plot and character; it was not a finished text, as most of Hardy's other books were by this stage (S. Gatrell, 1988, 101).

The serialization demanded plot development in each chapter, as in weekly TV soap operas. The serial *Graphic Tess* contained more sensational elements than the novel; or, more correctly, Thomas Hardy put in some of the more lurid scenes to spice up the instalments, and left them in the novel in the first edition and in following editions. In the *Life*, Hardy relates how the serial of *Tess of the d'Urbervilles* was rejected by *Murray's Magazine* and *Macmillan's Magazine*; so, before sending it to the third editor, of the *Graphic*, Hardy edited it. He took out the offending chapters, planning to publish them separately, and corrected the text (the scenes that were published separately in the *National Observer* and

Fortnightly Review were "Saturday Night in Arcady" and "The Midnight Baptism"). He 'carried out this unceremonious concession to conventionality with cynical amusement,' he says in the *Life*, 'knowing the novel was moral enough and to spare.' As he notes, the work was drudgery, and it might have been easier for him to have written a new story.

Other emendations Thomas Hardy made to the serial *Graphic* include the ennobling and purifying of Tess Durbeyfield's personality (see T. Wright, S. Gatrell, P. Boumelha, J. Laird). Tess's character in the revisions that Hardy made went through 'a process of refining, ennobling, and idealizing' (J. Laird, 1975, 125). She becomes more courageous and morally 'pure', more mature, less like a child. The rape was altered: Tess did not take Alec's 'cordial' before lying down. In the scene where she suckles her child, for example, the text originally said 'with a curious, stealthy movement, and rising of colour'. Hardy changed this to: 'with a curiously stealthy yet courageous movement, and with a still rising of colour' (XIV; J. Laird, 126). Hardy also made more of the d'Urberville inheritance, which further ennobled Tess, and added an extra dimension to her innate pride. The description of Tess's sexuality, early on in the novel, went through a number of alterations:

She was yawning, & he saw the red interior of her mouth
                                                                        had
                        so
as if it had been a snake's She stretched one naked arm high
                coiled-up cable of   its delicacy above the
sunburn;
above her head of twisted up hair that he could see almost to the shoulder
[?]
                was   with
her face been flushed from sleep, & her eyelids hung heavy over their pupils. It
incarnate
was a moment when a woman is more the flesh than at any other time;
                        beauty inclines to the
when the most spiritual is corporeal; & when sex takes the outside place

in her presentation. (folio 239-240; J. Laird, 64)

Tess's function as a 'victim', someone who's hunted, was enhanced by the symbolism that Thomas Hardy added at later stages: the mistletoe, the rat-hunt, the nests and traps, the altars and blood, the images of tombs and sacrifice. In the *Graphic* Hardy summarized Tess's time at Trantridge and the sham marriage thus:

> *"He made love to me, as you said he would do; and he asked me to marry him… I never liked him; but at last I agreed, knowing you'd be angry if I didn't. He said it must be private, even from you, on account of his mother; and by special licence; and foolishly I agreed to that likewise, to get rid of his pestering. I drove with him to Melchester, and there in a private room I went through the form of marriage with him as before a registrar. A few weeks after, I found that it was not the registrar's house we had gone to, as I had supposed, but the house of a friend of his, who had played the part of the registrar. I then came away from Trantridge instantly, though he wished me to stay; and here I am."* (*Graphic*, 136)

Feminist critics have noted how the narrator of *Tess of the d'Urbervilles* is himself deeply (sometimes jealously and ambiguously) in love with his heroine. The intensity of the reader's identification with Tess Durbeyfield can be seen in much of Hardy criticism. J. Hillis Miller, a respected Hardy critic, writes in *Fiction and Repetition*: 'I for one find the description of Angel Clare's failure to consummate his marriage to Tess almost unbearably painful' (1982, 119).

A couple of interconnected points are worth making about this revealing comment; firstly, it is that of a male critic, who is relating to a deeply sexualized female character – the intensity of the critic's identification may be related to the assumed gender of the critic and the character; secondly, the male critic assumes the significance of sexual consummation to be enormous. Sex is deemed crucial – it's 'unbearably painful' when Tess doesn't get the sexual consummation the critic thinks she desires.

One critic suggested that Thomas Hardy was so protective of

Tess Durbeyfield he deliberately had her keep her distance, sexually, from Angel Clare and Alec d'Urberville (a delightfully kookoo idea). For another critic, Hardy's identification with Tess, when it's so intense, can exonerate her of her mistakes (Laura Claridge in "Tess: A Less Than Pure Woman Ambivalently Presented", 324f). *Tess of the d'Urbervilles'* narrator may start out describing events from the detached position of a topographer or historian, but soon his disinterestedness is overtaken by an erotic gaze as he looks at Tess, isolates her from other clubwalkers, and describes her eyes and 'mobile peony mouth' (later on, Tess's eyes are described as having 'ever-varying pupils, with their radiating fibrils of blue, and black, and gray, and violet' XXVII).

> ...looking at Tess as she sat there, with her flower-like mouth and large tender eyes, neither black nor blue nor grey nor violet; rather all those shades together, and a hundred others, which could be seen if one looked into their irises – shade behind shade – tint beyond tint – around pupils that had no bottom; an almost standard woman, but for the slight incautiousness of character inherited from her race.

Alec's erotic gaze is the one that marks Tess, not Angel's, and this image of Tess – as eroticized and colonized by a vulgar, shallow male – becomes the basis of her image in the rest of the book. It is as if Alec imprinted his gaze on Tess first, not Angel (K. Silverman, 1984). Angel Clare did see her first – but not fully, only as a maiden standing slightly apart from the other dancers at Marlott. The narrator notes that it was sad that Angel did not connect with Tess first.

Part of the pressure of the narrator upon Tess Durbeyfield is phallic, with its tropes of penetration and piercing (the rosethorn, Prince's death, and so on). The narrator describes ways in to Tess's body – through her eyes, mouth and skin. For Penny Boumelha, the

> narrator's erotic fantasies of penetration and engulfment enact a pursuit, violation and persecution of Tess in parallel with those she suffers at the hands of her two lovers. (1982, 120)

The authorial pressure upon Tess Durbeyfield, and especially upon her body, make her 'not just discursively determined, but discursively *overdetermined*', as Kaja Silverman put it in "History, Figuration and Female Subjectivity in *Tess of the d'Urbervilles*". Hardy's texts are 'over-determined', J. Hillis Miller noted, due to their 'too many irreconcilable' elements (1982, 128).

For feminist critics, the important parts of the book Thomas Hardy changed over different editions were Tess's character. Tess was originally called Sue, Love, Cis and also Rose Mary. She was called Love Woodrow, Cis Woodrow and sometimes Sue Troublewell. She was later Rose-Mary Troublefield. The name d'Urberville was originally 'Hawnferne' (it become 'Turberville' before it became 'd'Urberville').

Early titles for the novel were *Too Late Beloved,* and *Too Late, Beloved!,* and also *The Body and Soul of Sue*, when Thomas Hardy was contemplating calling Tess Sue (he used the name in *Jude the Obscure*). The resonance of the phrase 'too late beloved' occurs in the Sandbourne scene in the later part, when Angel Clare returns. Tess spoke standard English rather than the dialect, which was added later (H, 19). She became more and more significant for Hardy, it seems, as her 'innocence' and 'chastity' were emphasized. She was 'purified' – 'Tess's purity... is "stuck on"', says Mary Jacobus in "Tess's Purity" (78). Hardy apparently made the differences between Alec and Tess more extreme – they were more like 'equals' in earlier versions of the story.

In one view, Tess Durbeyfield herself brings together most of Thomas Hardy's women characters: the submissive type, the 'flirt', the *femme fatale*, the 'victim', the idealistic lover, and the would-be teacher or educated woman (P. Boumelha, 1982, 117). Tess is exalted, at various times, as a poet, as a martyr, as a saint (during the baptism), as a religious rebel (again, at the baptism, and afterwards with Angel), as an archetypal 'fallen woman', as a sensuous nature lover, as a fecund Goddess.

There is Tess Durbeyfield the would-be school teacher; Tess the 'milkmaid'; Tess the worker; Tess the 'wronged maiden' of balladry; Tess the 'good-girl, governness-type heroine of Victorian convention' (E. Moers, 1967); there is Tess the unconventional single mother; Tess the murderer; Tess the 'victim'; Tess the prostitute; Tess the proto-New Woman; Tess the Earth Mother; and Tess the aristocratic d'Urberville, doomed, romantic, noble, yet enduring (Ellen Moers says this stereotype 'may have been Hardy's favourite' [1967]).

The title page of *Tess of the d'Urbervilles* is usually printed thus:

TESS OF THE D'URBERVILLES

A PURE WOMAN
FAITHFULLY PRESENTED BY THOMAS HARDY

*'...Poor wounded name! My bosom as a bed
Shall lodge thee.'* – W. Shakespeare

The sub-title is now infamous, particularly the emphasis on Tess Durbeyfield as a 'pure woman' (critics such as J. Goode, 1988, M. Jacobus, 1976, and others, have analyzed Thomas Hardy's ambiguous use of the term 'pure'). But the novel is, partly, about the question that Tess Durbeyfield puts to herself in 'Phase the Second: Maiden No More': '[w]as once lost always lost really true of chastity?' (XV). Of Tess's 'purity', Hardy told Edmund Blunden that 'her innate purity remained intact to the very last; though I frankly own that a certain outward purity left her on her last fall' (E. Blunden, 1942).

Many editions of *Tess of the d'Urbervilles* will tell the reader that the William Shakespeare quote comes from *Two Gentlemen of Verona* (I. ii. 115-6). The quote links together language and love (the textuality of sex, in postmodern lingo), with the trope of nurturing the beloved's name in the bed of the heart. The other emphasis is on the name of the beloved being 'wounded'. As critics have noted, the character Tess was particularly cherished by Thomas Hardy, so it is right that the title page quote should refer to a desire to care for the *name* of the beloved (Tess as a character), rather than Tess 'herself'. The implication is that, despite being 'wounded', as Tess Durbeyfield is, the loved one will still be cherished.

It is not so much the meaning of the quote that counts on the title page of *Tess of the d'Urbervilles* as the fact that it is William Shakespeare, without question (English) literature's god. Two sources will guarantee a measure of weightiness if one slaps them on one's title page: Shakespeare and the *Bible*.

Thomas Hardy, of course, used both sources profusely, quoting from them or alluding to them throughout his fiction and poetry. *Tess of the d'Urbervilles* is particularly rich in Biblical allusions, such as *Exodus* (13, 20: 5), *Jonah* (4: 6-7), *Psalms* (9, 31, 102), *1 Kings* (18:7), *Genesis* (3: 16), *Ezekiel* (23), *Ecclesiastes* (3: 5), the Sermon on the Mount, *Acts* (17: 28), *Revelations* (22: 1), *Proverbs* (21: 9, 25: 34), *John* (13: 27), and of course the many allusions to the writings of St Paul. Tess's pain is compared to that of Job; she is seen as the Queen of Sheba adoring Solomon (Angel Clare), a reference to the *Song of Songs*, which was later central to *Jude the Obscure*; the elder Clare is compared to Abraham, with Angel as a misnamed Isaac; and so on.

Laura Claridge in a *Texas Studies in Literature and Language* article has seen the narrator's Biblical commentary as undermining Tess Durbeyfield's characterization: she is supposed, for example, to be 'charitable', and demands charity from both Alec d'Urberville and Angel Clare, yet is not charitable herself. The Shakespearean allusions in *Tess* include, obviously, tragedies such as *Macbeth, King Lear* and *Hamlet,* and also *Twelfth Night, Measure For Measure, Romeo and Juliet,* and so on.

Critics have also seized upon another aspect of Thomas Hardy's subtitle: 'a pure woman faithfully *presented*': the emphasis on (re)presentation echoes through critical theories such as post-structuralism and post-Lacanian psychoanalysis. In this critical view, Tess Durbeyfield is 'presented', that is, mediated by visualizations, her existence is via appearance only. She is 'presented', also, because she is largely seen from outside, via her body (her eyes, mouth, and so on), while her inner life remains unknowable, because it is unseen (P. Widdowson, 1993, 19). Tess becomes an unknowable character; she is a series of images, of other people's images of her, she doesn't have an 'essence' but is a collection of representations (M. Humm, 1995, 37), as Alec and Angel idealize her or sexualize her, her mother sees her as a pretty advert to gain help with the family's poverty, society sees her as an outsider, and the narrator fetishizes her. When Tess picks up the corn the narrator says she embraces it like a lover (XIV).

The 'Tess' that Angel Clare creates – the virginal, pure, faithful, mythical country maiden – stands in for the purity and spotlessness that's missing from his life. However, the flesh-and-blood Tess, the 'real' Tess, disrupts this imagined, longed-for purity. Her presence confirms the lack of spotlessness in Angel's life. The May Day clubwalking announces the theme of erotic looking in *Tess of the d'Urbervilles*: the narrator gazes erotically at Tess through the Angel's gaze as he looks back at Tess. The narrator is aroused by Tess's look and 'tropes her actions as sexual and inviting violation' (D. Sadoff, 151).

'SHE FELT AKIN TO THE LANDSCAPE': *TESS'S* SYMBOLISM

Tess of the d'Urbervilles is regarded as Thomas Hardy's great novel of human-nature integration.[1] Despite being crude and cartoon-like at times, Hardy's use of setting and symbolism is very powerful. *Tess of the d'Urbervilles* would lose much if it lost its settings. The earth itself becomes a narrative force – from the pastoral languor of the Vale of Marlott with its pagan customs (the May Day dance, I. ii), Tess Durbeyfield moves to the unknown lands of Trantridge. She knows it is a strange place, because strawberries are already in season there (V). She is raped among 'the primæval yews and oaks of The Chase', in total darkness (XI). After her dazed time with Alec d'Urberville (XII), she returns to her homeland a changed person. She retreats into herself, nursing her bruised body and soul. But she is resilient – indomitable. She is still alive and open to experiences. From her bedroom window

> *under her few square yards of thatch, she watched winds and snows, and rains, gorgeous sunsets, and successive moons at their full... She knew how to hit to a hair's-breadth that moment of evening when the light and darkness are so evenly balanced that the constraint of day and the suspense of night neutralize each other, leaving absolute mental liberty... On those lonely hills and dales her quiescent glide was of a piece with the element she moved in. Her flexuous and stealthy figure became an integral part of the scene. At times her whimsical fancy would intensify natural processes around her till they seemed part of her own story. (44)*

This's actually a depiction of Tess Durbeyfield's pregnancy. *Tess of the d'Urbervilles* opens with a pastoral vision of Wessex. Yet it is worth remembering that Tess herself thinks she is living on a 'blighted planet'. Even in her youthful, innocent phase, she is cynical (or realist). She does not expect to be given anything by her world. But it does give her this vision of Wessex, one of Thomas Hardy's finest evocations of his beloved country:

> *The traveller...is surprised and delighted to behold, extended like a map before him, a country differing absolutely from that which he has passed through. Behind him the hills are open, the sun blazes down upon fields so large as to give an unenclosed character to the landscape, the lanes are white, the hedges low and plashed, the atmosphere colourless... The atmosphere is languorous, and is so tinged with azure that what artists call the middle distance partakes also of that hue, while the horizon behind is of the deepest ultramarine. (II)*

This is a painterly vision. Thomas Hardy invites the reader to see the country as a landscape painter might. The colours – azure, ultramarine – are the most precious hues of the Renaissance (blue was more expensive than gold). This is a rich vision, rich in coveted azure, a vista drenched in the glow of lapis lazuli. It recalls the Arcadian views of Claude Lorrain. The last time the reader sees Tess Durbeyfield is at Stonehenge. The trajectory of her tragedy is embodied in these two landscapes – the beginning is so soft, languid, pastoral, Tess so fully at home within it. The ending at Stonehenge is so dark, hesitant, reserved. She is sleeping on the sacrifical stone, a stained victim. The two landscapes tell the reader as much about her experience as the plot or the characters.

As Jude Fawley in *Jude the Obscure* is the 'natural boy', so Tess Durbeyfield is the natural girl, fully enmeshed with nature, with her surroundings. She embodies nature and nature is the embodiment of her. Tess, though a country girl, a provincial character, is nevertheless explicitly described as a Great Mother Goddess. She is at various moments a Saint, a Mystic, a Philosopher, a Poet, a Whore and a Slave. Tess is seen as a Goddess, for, as 'woman', she is identical with nature and the earth. The seasons flow through her. Her story is the story of nature, except that Tess's tragic end stems not from a failure of nature but from the failure of her men to really see her for what she really is.[2]

It is the women in *Tess of the d'Urbervilles*, not the men, who are fully in harmony with the landscape. Women become part of nature, while men build machines that move across the surface, scratching away at nature's skin. Men treat nature like dirt – they build the trains, threshing-machines and so on, which divorce people from the soil. The field-women, however, assimilate themselves with their environment (XIV).

Talbothays and its surroundings is not as beautiful as Marlott Vale, but is 'more cheering' (XVI). Here there is a

> *change in the quality of the air from heavy to light, or the sense of being amid new scenes where there were no invidious eyes upon her, sent up her spirits wonderfully. Her hopes mingled with the sunshine in an ideal photosphere which surrounded her as she bounded along against the soft south wind. She heard a pleasant voice in every breeze, and in every bird's*

note seemed to lurk a joy. (XVI)

Here Tess blossoms. The Midsummer dawn trysts are some of Thomas Hardy's most celebrated passages. Sexuality and nature are fused. Blood and passion are heated up in the sun (XXIV). Tess is a rich liver of life – 'Hardy's Tess is a sexually vital consciousness' (R. Morgan, 1988, 84) – '"she lives what paper-poets only write"', says Angel Clare (XXVI), admitting covertly his own inadequacies (and that of all writers). Angel distances himself, while Tess moves in closer. She really lives.

After the awful honeymoon night, Thomas Hardy is none too subtle in his symbolism and *mise-en-scène*. Angel Clare is thus confronted by the ashes from the fire. The same sledgehammer symbolism occurs when Tess Durbeyfield compassionately kills the maimed pheasants (XLI). Pheasants, those soft, plump and beautiful birds, the targets of men of leisure (they are bred in Britain for the sole, grotesque purpose of being shot by middle-class men), will later bring Connie and Mellors together in D.H. Lawrence's last novel, *Lady Chatterley's Lover*.

> *Under the trees several pheasants lay about, their rich plumage dabbled with blood; some were dead, some feebly twitching a wing, some staring up at the sky, some pulsating quickly, some contorted, some stretched out – all of them writhing in agony, except the fortunate ones whose tortures had ended during the night by the inability of nature to bear more.*

Flintcomb-Ash, with its frozen fields, speaks for itself. Tess's long, gruelling walk to Emminster is heart-rending. It is fully described – for here Thomas Hardy can pull together many places in his beloved Dorset. The work on the threshing-machine is also exhausting. Tess Durbeyfield is an immensely active protagonist – she is not a disaffected wanderer, like many of the characters in the fiction of, say, Aldous Huxley, Evelyn Waugh and E.M. Forster, and she is not a lazy bohemian, as in J.-K. Huysmans. She is a helluva worker.

The degradation continues, as Tess Durbeyfield and her family camp outside King's Bere church. Thomas Hardy's comparison of the family on the bed outside and their ancestors in their tombs inside the church is again crude, but it does the trick. It is a brutal contrast – the family so alive, fleshy, hungry and poor on one side of the wall, and the knightly forebears once spiritually and financially rich, but now materially just useless dust on the other side. Much of the novel uses spatial *mise-en-scène*: Tess placed in the coffin by Angel; Tess happening to pass the preaching Alec. Hardy loves orchestrating his series of accidents and coincidences.

Tess Durbeyfield adrift in Sandbourne (inspired partly by Bournemouth), is Tess fully displaced. She is a real outsider, a stranger to this lazy life of finery and hanging about in hotels. There is nothing for her to do. She is in a town, disconnected from nature. The setting is a town with no history, a place dedicated to leisure and retirement, not to labour (Bournemouth and Poole is now the one of the largest non-industrial connurbations in Europe). This is all Alec can offer her – sex and money. The modern world has already overcome all things natural and spontaneous, with this dead tourist centre.

The irony of Stonehenge, with all its links with the past, with ancient weather- and star-watching people, with the whole of paganism, is a bitter irony. It is obvious and clumsy, this Stonehenge setting, yet Thomas Hardy brings it off (the word 'Stonehenge' only occurs once in the whole book).

'It is Stonehenge!' said Clare.
'The heathen temple, you mean?'

There is the suggestions of a mythic return to the paganism of the opening pages – the May club-walking or dance – a suggestion that life is cyclical. But Stonehenge is bleak – exposed to the elements, desolate. It is a site of death, a temple to the dead as much as to the sun. The solar power of Stonehenge is dead now – it cannot save Tess. There is no escape in the ancient past, or, symbolized by Wintonchester, in the Middle Ages.

With Win(ton)chester the narrative returns to the old capital of Wessex. Tess Durbeyfield's many journeys have led her to this old centre. Thomas Hardy's narrator cleverly introduces the city as a historic and beautiful place – 'The city of Wintoncester, that fine old city, aforetime capital of Wessex, lay amidst its convex and concave downlands in all the brightness and warmth of a July morning' (LIX). He then goes on to describe the modern red-brick gaol, rising in front of the old city, the new structures displacing the old ones. In the same way the train is compared with the figure of Tess. The railroad invades the countryside, superimposing itself upon the ancient landscape. So the new, the harshly modern and industrial, is not integrated with the old and the traditional, but simply thrown down upon it. Other uses of spatial *mise-en-scène* in *Tess of the d'Urbervilles* includes the threshing-machine; the empty house where Angel and Tess hide (contrasting with the Sandbourne hotel); the coffin; the Cross-in-Hand and so on.

May Day, which opens *Tess of the d'Urbervilles*, is crammed full of folklore and poetic associations. It is associated with fertility, sexuality, trees, flowers, bonfires and all things pagan. May Day Goddesses include Flora, Maia, Luna, Asherah, Danu and Tanit. May Eve is the German Walpurgisnacht, the night of witches, orgies, drinking, dancing and the Celtic bonfire feast of Beltane. There is a May Queen and King, dancing among the sacred oak trees. In England, the Morris-men, flouncing about with their scarves and bells, seem ridiculous – what a national dance! Yet their dances and games are all about fertility and sexuality, and, at times, with their use of scapegoats, Morris-dancing uses ritual violence. (Of course, May Day has other associations – left-wing and socialist political ones, for instance – it is known as Labour Day and International Workers' Day).

No wonder, then, that Thomas Hardy uses these festival days, with their fusion of sex, love, fertility, magic, nature and Goddess cults, involving the whole community. It is significant that he focuses on women in these rituals (in *Tess, The Woodlanders* and

The Return of the Native, especially). Chapter Two in *Tess of the d'Urbervilles* moves from the long shot descriptions of the 'fertile and sheltered tract of country' (p. 48 – the adjectives could apply also to Tess Durbeyfield herself), to the history of the place. The May Day dance is introduced by reference to the ancient forests of the region (Hardy is accurate here as ever, for Maytime rituals are bound up with tree-worship, symbolized by the Maypole). Hardy then describes the Cerealian sisterhood of the girls' club-walking. In invoking Ceres, Hardy makes his village maidens latterday upholders of a Goddess cult. There are strong undertones of matriarchy here, of feminine ritual and vitality. Indeed, the images of female solidarity are one of the most uplifting parts of the novel: Tess and her friends are set against the barren spirituality of Angel Clare and his brothers; Tess and the milkmaids; Tess later on, down-trodden, finding sanctuary with Miriam.

As Ovid says, at the Ceres festival white is the main colour. White is Tess Durbeyfield's colour – white plus red: purity stained with red blood.[3] Thomas Hardy evokes the scene vividly and with thinly veiled eroticism. The wisdom of the grandmothers and crones adds to the dimension of witchcraft. But the narrator's interest is in those 'under whose bodices the life throbbed quick and warm.' (II). These girls dance alone. They do not need men. When the men arrive, they only offer dissatisfaction. It is a crisis time for Tess, so pure and virginal yet so cynical too, and so aggressively described by her creator – she has a red ribbon, hot blushes and a 'pouted-up deep red mouth' (II).

If only Angel Clare could have made the connection with Tess Durbeyfield at the beginning. But it was 'too late'. Tess, with life and its red-blooded passions overtaking her, is harvested not by her true soul-mate, but by one who is only interested in her blossoming body. The pagan-Christian conflict is so rigorously brought out in this opening scene, as are the other themes of sexual maturity versus virginity, and youth versus old age, and ignorance versus experience – unknowing (in Tess) and wisdom (in the old women).

Thomas Hardy made everything relatively clear in *Tess of the d'Urbervilles* – he did not make the main parts of the story deliberately mysterious. For example, Hardy's use of symbolism is pretty rough. For instance, Alec d'Urberville says '"my arms [are] a lion rampant"' (V). Instead of saying the d'Urberville heraldic arms are a rampant lion Hardy might as well have said a rampant phallus, 'all the better to eat you with', as the wolf says to Little Red Riding Hood.

From the very first description of Tess Durbeyfield, she is eroticized by the narrator. As the all-seeing, voyeuristic eye of the narrator roves over the sisterhood of club-walkers, it closes in and rests on Tess, drawing attention to her 'mobile peony mouth' (II). The eroticization of Tess's mouth and body occurs partly because Thomas Hardy cannot depict sex acts, so his narrator displaces attention to Tess's body, descriptions which can get past the censor. In doing so, Tess's erotic body is simultaneously exalted and suppressed, spoken and silenced. As Mary Jacobus puts it, '[t]hough Hardy seems to be salvaging Tess's body for spirituality (the vessel is brim-full), the yawning mouth opens up a split in the very terms he uses' (1986, 31).

Like many male narrators, *Tess of the d'Urbervilles'* narrator is fascinated by what is inside Tess's body, the great unknown of Freudian psychoanalysis – that is, female sexuality. The problem is that, as French feminists such as Luce Irigaray and Hélène Cixous noted, female sexuality is unrepresentable in patriarchal culture. Thus, the closer Thomas Hardy's narrator gets to Tess's erotic interior, the less can be said about it. Instead, Tess's body becomes part of the male narcissistic process, that is, a mirror in which men see their narcissism reflected. (Not only Angel and Alec see their narcissism reflected in Tess, but also Tess's father, with his dream of her continuing the d'Urberville heritage, and other male characters). As Margaret Higonnet asks of *Tess*, '[c]an a man implicated in patriarchy speak for a woman constrained by it?'[4]

'AN EMOTION THRUST ON THEM BY CRUEL NATURE'S LAW': NATURE VERSUS CULTURE

The 'tragedy' of *Tess of the d'Urbervilles* cannot be averted, it seems. Once the wheels of destiny are in motion, nothing can stop them. Jack Durbeyfield learning he's really a d'Urberville is where the novel begins: this is what sets the course of events in motion which has Tess Durbeyfield going to Trantridge. However, the reader can think up alternative plots. For example, if John Durbeyfield had met Parson Tringham by chance one more time, the following day or so, he might have asked about the d'Urbervilles who lived at The Slopes. Parson Tringham would then have told him they were fake d'Urbervilles, and really Stokes. Consequently, Joan Durbeyfield's 'projick' of sending Tess to claim kin might have been dropped. Thus Tess Durbeyfield might never have met Alec. In Thomas Hardy's world, though, something just as bad would have befallen her. After all, *before* she even goes to Trantridge she accidentally kills the family's horse, which they rely on heavily (another rather unbelievable event). Even before she meets Alec, she regards herself as a murderess. Thus, if it wasn't Alec she met, there would be someone else, if the narrative had progressed otherwise. Meeting Angel without having been raped by Alec would make the novel quite different.

An alternative narrative for *Tess of the d'Urbervilles*, then, might see the honeymoon scene between Tess and Angel as before: but this time, Tess would be much upset by Angel's confession of his erotic 'dissipation'. Tess would probably have forgiven Angel, but the sexual politics of the novel would have a different slant. Continuing this alternative *Tess of the d'Urbervilles* further (one of many that could be conceived), Angel would eventually become bored with Tess. Like Edred Fitzpiers in *The Woodlanders*, Angel would still cherish Tess but would start looking elsewhere. The resulting story, of male adultery and women putting up with it, would be far less interesting than *Tess of the d'Urbervilles* as it stands.

Tess of the d'Urbervilles takes the breaking of a social law and develops it as a number of ricochets. The initial rape develops into narratives concerning having sex before marriage, having a child outside wedlock, trying to live outside of society and Christianity, lying to one's betrothed, living in sin, and finally murder. Religion is not automatically dominant in the rural community, though: as one critic put it, 'although almost all the characters attend church [in *Tess*], they do not believe in or understand Christian dogma' (N. Schoenburg, 1989).

The text opposes culture with nature: the narrator seems to be on the side of nature. Culture, embodied in Angel Clare's ardent religiosity and Alec's fake knowledge, is dangerous. It upsets the time-honoured equilibrium of the rural world. Nature is prized above culture, perhaps, because it seems to be more in tune with life. Though it is the men who are often the culture bearers, it is the women who actually yearn more, are more socially ambitious (as also in D.H. Lawrence's novels, such as *The Rainbow*, which's a kind of sequel to *Tess*). What men offer in Thomas Hardy's texts is a cultural sophistication which, finally, the women, not the men, do not want. Tess Durbeyfield, at one of her lowpoints, repeats to herself that '[a]ll is vanity'. However, she goes on to consider that '[a]ll was, alas, worse than vanity – injustice, punishment, exaction, death' (XLI):

> *Was there another such a wretched being as she in the world? Tess asked herself; and, thinking of her wasted life, said, 'All is vanity.' She repeated the words mechanically, till she reflected that this was a most inadequate thought for modern days. Solomon had thought as far as that more than two thousand years ago; she herself, though not in the van of thinkers, had got much further. If all were only vanity, who would mind it? All was, alas, worse than vanity – injustice, punishment, exaction, death.*

Nature is not free from pain and complications in Thomas Hardy's fictive world: in fact, everything hurts. Love, marriage, work, religion, nature – all have pain. In the *Life*, Hardy wrote:

'[p]ain has been, and pain is' (315). The women in the Talbothays bedroom writhe 'feverishly under the oppressiveness of an emotion thrust on them by cruel Nature's law' (XXIII). But pain = being alive in the Western (masculinist) tradition, and the most exquisite sort of suffering in Hardy's fictive realm is being in love. Love = pain = life. The point about Tess is that she is fully alive: 'she *lives* what paper-poets write' (XXVI). Tess is seen as being more fully alive than the male characters in the narrative.

The exaltation of women in the 1891 novel, though, is double-edged. Tess Durbeyfield embodies much that men exalt in women, and she suffers because of it. Tess, for example, deliberately makes herself ugly, to escape the lecherous looks of men (XLII). Ironically, when Tess is deprived of Angel's gaze, she slips into melancholy. Angel's allegorizing (and erotic) gaze is important in stabilizing Tess's self-image.)[5] Tess lives fully in her body, but Alec indulges his negligently, and Angel is scarcely aware of his (he brushes aside the discomforts of his Brazilian adventure). What Angel demands and Tess cannot deliver is the pure, idealized body. Tess's body goes through much: rape, pregnancy, childbirth, her child's death, labouring and travelling.

Tess of the d'Urbervilles is a problematic novel, gender-wise, because 'Hardy appears to lay much of the blame for [Tess's] difficulties on the body' (L. Pykett). Julia Kristeva's reading of the Christian Crucifixion is pertinent to the sense of bodily suffering in Thomas Hardy's heroines (in particular Tess Durbeyfield). For Kristeva, writing in *Tales of Love*, the moment of agony in the Crucifixion and its immediate aftermath is usefully regarded in terms of a psychoanalytic feminism:

> *Since resurrection there is, and, as Mother of God, she must know this, nothing justifies Mary's outburst of pain at the foot of the cross, unless it be the desire to experience within her own body the death of a human being, which her feminine fate of being the source of life spares her. Could it be that love, as puzzling as it is ancient, of mourners for corpses relates to the same longing of a woman whom nothing fulfills – the longing to experience*

the wholly masculine pain of a man who expires at every moment on account of jouissance due to obsession with his own death? And yet, Marian pain is in no way connected with tragic outburst: joy and even a kind of triumph follow upon tears, as if the conviction that death does not exist were an irrational but unshakable maternal certainty, on which the principle of resurrection had to rest. (250-1)

Both men in *Tess of the d'Urbervilles* have fantasies about their self-image. Alec d'Urberville plays the part of a fake aristocrat, using capital gained from manufacturing; Angel Clare imagines he can (like Clym Yeobright in *The Return of the Native*) move down a class or two and help on a working class farm (P. Boumelha, 1982, 43). Angel also has fantasies that Tess Durbeyfield is nothing more than a simple country girl.

Tess's suffering can be seen as out of proportion with her mistakes or 'crimes'. After the rape and sorrowful motherhood, 'as Thomas Hardy sees it, there is no reason in nature for Tess Durbeyfield to receive further punishment' (B. Sankey, 1965; A. LaValley, 95). Yet she does. Because there are no 'reasons' in nature. Punishment is not about nature; paying for crimes only occurs in humans. The 'causes' of Tess's tragedy, seen within the narrative, in terms of events, often seem trivial or at least relatively minor. For example, one of the 'causes' for Tess to climb up with Alec on his horse before the rape is her argument with Car Darch. Tess's d'Urberville pride asserts itself here, as she tries to raise herself above the workers. But Tess's mistake at this point, to try to keep aloof, is not commensurate with her subsequent 'punishment', her rape.

In *Tess of the d'Urbervilles*, sham marriages (Alec d'Urberville and Tess Durberyfield) are followed by legal but sexually/spiritually damaged marriages (Angel and Tess), then another legal marriage (Alec and Tess, a trick marriage, not desired by Tess), then the spiritual and sexual consummation in the empty house. One 'marriage' ironically and ambivalently modulates the one before. The narrative reads something like this: '(Unconsummated) marriage > (adulterous) "marriage" > (Alec's) death >

(consummated) marriage > (Tess's) death > (Angel's implied re-(marriage', as Dianne Sadoff put it in "Looking at Tess: The Female Figure in Two Narrative Media" (156).

RIGHT PLACE, WRONG TIME

Tess Durbeyfield is Thomas Hardy's most accomplished female character in many ways. She is identified with nature, fertility, growth, the seasons and Goddesses. The men, though, are not gods: they are not even fairy tale princes, or aristocrats. Angel Clare is a would-be Christ, but Tess surpasses him in that role. Alec and Angel are simply not up to Tess: she is their superior. While her suitors live fragmentarily in their souls or bodies, Tess lives in her soul and body, and lustily, wholly. The men are fragments; Tess is whole, even at her lowest ebb, at Flintcomb Ash.

Thomas Hardy's poem 'Tess's Lament' offers a different way of apportioning 'blame' from the novel:

And it was I who did it all,
  Who did it all;
'Twas I who made the blow to fall
  On him who thought no guile.
Well, it is finished – past, and he
has left me to my misery,
And I must take my Cross on me
  For wronging him awhile. (CP, 176)

The tragedy of *Tess of the d'Urbervilles* is partly that the 'right man' comes at the 'wrong time' (V). This is one of Thomas Hardy's defining novelistic structures. Hardyan irony pivots around 'right place, wrong time', or vice versa, the 'if only' of fate, destiny, chance, time and circumstance (J. Brooks, 12).

Wrong place, right time; or right place, wrong time. Tess

Durbeyfield, after all, is ready for a tender, affectionate, considerate love when she goes to Alec d'Urberville's house and meets Alec instead of Angel Clare. *Tess*'s narrator remarks that it's a pity that Tess did not meet Angel earlier. This might not have been successful either, for Angel shows himself to be markedly more immature than Tess: if Angel had met Tess at age 16, as she was at the beginning of the novel, he would probably have still have made a mess of their relationship. Tess though, would have been able to extricate herself from his clutches relatively easily, much easier than it was to deal with Angel years later, as with Alec. There is no one to 'blame' for the cruelty of chance/ fate/ fortune/ circumstance/ time. There are circumstances which are simply difficult, which Hardy calls 'the harrowing contingencies of human experience, the unexpectedness of things' (XXXV).

Scapegoats are required, though. '"Once victim, always victim – that's the law"' (XLVII).

> 'Now, punish me!' she said, turning up her eyes to him with the hopeless defiance of the sparrow's gaze before its captor twists its neck. 'Whip me, crush me; you need not mind those people under the rick! I shall not cry out. Once victim, always victim – that's the law!'

The point is that *all* the people in *Tess of the d'Urbervilles* are victims. It is just not Tess Durbeyfield who is trapped into a certain way of thinking and acting, but also Alec, Angel, Mrs Durbeyfield, Farmer Groby, and so on. There is spontaneity, freedom, nature, but such openness is continually crushed by socialized ways of thinking and doing. Tess retains her openness and potential, even at the end, which is why she is a 'pure woman'. She still believes in happiness at the end of the novel, astonishingly. She is indomitable. She speaks of the 'sweet and lovely' time she and Angel Clare have in the empty house (LVIII). She knows, too, as she wakes up on the sacrifical stone at Stonehenge, that '[t]his happiness could not have lasted' (LVIII). Though a 'victim', Tess experiences rapture, is loved and loathed, is perhaps the most alive of Thomas Hardy's characters.

Tess Durbeyfield is a scandalous figure, as far as Victorian society was concerned.[6] She is offensive to Victorian sensibility – she is raped, she lives in sin and adultery, she is openly sexual, a religious sceptic, and finally, a murderer (K. Blake, 1982, 690). Yet she is 'pure': Thomas Hardy bids the reader remember 'the meaning of the word in Nature' and the æsthetic and Christian uses of the term 'pure' (T, 38). By 'pure', Hardy means honest – she is true to herself. It is when the word 'pure' is associated with openly sexual and transgressive behaviour that the problems begin with such a definition.

TESS OF THE D'URBERVILLES AS FAIRY TALE

Tess of the d'Urbervilles is a proto-feminist text in its challenging of societal norms. It rewrites the 'wronged maiden' ballad narrative,[7] the fairy tale quality of the text, where the princess must marry her prince at the end. Hardy's *Tess* recalls *Little Red Riding Hood, Bluebeard* and *Sleeping Beauty*. Other similarities between *Tess of the d'Urbervilles* and *Little Red Riding Hood*: in a country setting a mother sends her young, virginal daughter on an errand to an old woman; both Tess and Little Red Riding Hood are marked by the colour red: (Tess has a red ribbon, strawberries, roses, blood, and so on); like the wolf, Alec diverts Tess's attention with masses of flowers; Alec acts like the wolf, with his predatory manner, his 'bold rolling eye' and sly, patronizing language ('Well, my Beauty', 'my pretty Coz'); as in *Little Riding Hood*, the food Tess eats 'in a half-pleased, half-reluctant state' (V) hints at sexual acts.

Other affinities between Thomas Hardy's fiction and fairy tales include: poverty; the rural settings; the weak father (in *Hansel and Gretel*); the dark forest; the Stoke-d'Urberville mansion as a (fake) fairy tale castle; older women envying young female beauty (in *The Woodlanders* and *Snow White*); family curses; potential violence; and the dream of perfect romance.

As in *Little Red Riding Hood,* a forest features prominently in *Tess of the d'Urbervilles*: the 'tragic' event in Tess Durbeyfield's relations with Alec d'Urberville, the rape, occurs in a forest. And not just any forest, but one of England's ancient woodlands, significantly known as The Chase. Tess is seen by the narrator as a prey to the hunter, as virgin or conquerable territory to the soldier, as a victim to the sadist, and as a sacrifical lamb to society (D. Sadoff, 156). The theme of hunting is evoked a number of times by the narrator,[8] not least in portraying Alec as a mock-squire predator. Even before the Trantridge episodes, Hardy's narrator in chapter two describes this part of Dorset as the Vale of the White Hart. The casually related anecdote of a mediæval legend, about a hunter killing 'a beautiful white hart' that was spared by Henry III and being fined for it, is of course not at all casual, but bears directly on Tess's fate. The identification between the hunted hart and hunted woman (the soft, white female object penetrated by the phallic axe or spear) also chimes with *Snow White and the Seven Dwarfs* (and has been used elsewhere many times).

Like fairy tales, *Tess of the d'Urbervilles* is full of sexual symbols, some of them hidden, others, like the strawberry, are obvious. In the opening chapters Alec d'Urberville comes out of a 'dark triangular door'; he gives Tess strawberries and roses, emblems of female sexuality (as with the roses in *Jude the Obscure*); Tess Durbeyfield is pricked and bleeds from a rose thorn; the blood from the dying horse gushes over her (there's no mere coincidence in Prince's name, nor in the gender of the horse); there's the lion rampant on the d'Urberville seal, and so on. Tess breaks a taboo, like the women in *Bluebeard*. Like Bluebeard's brides, Tess is soon covered in blood. However, unlike fairy tale heroines, Tess is marked by blood even before she embarks on the fateful journey to Trantridge, when Prince the horse dies. Thus, even before the rape or ill omens such as the rose thorn pricking her chin (VI), Tess regards 'herself in the light of a murderess' (IV). It's significant that only thirty pages into the book, at the end of chapter four, Tess is already thinking in terms of being a murderer.

In *Tess of the d'Urbervilles*, though, the heroine is beatified, and her beatification comes partly from her social transgressions. In *Tess of the d'Urbervilles*, many of the faults and mistakes come from men, from masculine discourses, and from patriarchal institutions, such as marriage and the Church. Tess (naïvely it turns out) expects to find a decently behaved human being who will return her love. What she gets is one man who rapes her and dominates her socially and psychologically, and another man who cannot accept all of her, her past, her body and sexuality, her desires. Tess asks too much of her suitors: she wishes for too much as a fairy tale princess: she wishes for love. She gives love, time after time, but receives a jaundiced, selfish, fetishized sort of love in return.

In *The Newly Born Woman*, what Hélène Cixous writes about intention and desire applies directly to Tess Durbeyfield's fate: '[i]ntention: desire, authority – examine them and you are led right back...to the father.' So that '[e]ither woman is passive or she does not exist. What is left of her is unthinkable, unthought' (1994, 39). Cytherea Graye is also 'passive', remaining throughout much of *Desperate Remedies* in a constrained position. When Tess returns to her mother and cries '"[w]hy didn't you tell me there was danger in men-folk?"' (XII), it is a terribly direct question. It is the sort of question one finds in Arthurian romance (such as 'what do women want?' – 'sovereignty' was Georges Bataille's suggestion). Tess's question goes to the heart of Thomas Hardy's theme (the inhumanity of humanity), and to the heart of feminism. Intolerance is his great theme, as with feminists such as Andrea Dworkin, Mary Daly, Susan Griffin and Luce Irigaray.

Tess Durbeyfield's mother is called 'simple', a 'poor witless wife' (VI). In fact, it is, ironically, very much Tess's mother who encourages Tess to go off to Trantridge to claim kin. One of the twists of the plot that Tess's mother inadvertently encourages is to make Tess attractive before she goes to Trantridge, so that she looks more mature than the 'maiden' she actually is. Joan Durbeyfield's plan works, and Tessfield becomes womanly, ahead of her years. Alec, then, does not see the 'real' Tess, but a dressed-up, manufactured Tess. Tess is again a 'tex' or text, upon which people inscribe their desires.

The narrator contrasts the two in terms of culture and language: the mother speaking the dialect, the daughter being able to speak 'ordinary English' (III) – the mother is two hundred years behind Tess Durbeyfield's education (III); the mother being content largely to stay at home as a 'housewife' and mother, the daughter musing on greater things. It is Joan Durbeyfield who consults the *Compleat Fortune-teller*, an object so potent she won't even allow it to remain in the house (a humorous send-up of rural superstition). It is Tess's mother who encourages her husband to consider her 'projick', who has the children back her up when Tess's unsure of going, who dresses Tess up in her best clothes on the day of departure.

Joan Durbeyfield is optimistic enough (or naïve enough) to hope that there is a decent man out there for her daughter to marry: similarly, when she wed Jack Durbeyfield she did not think he would take to sitting around and drinking (nobody hopes for that when they marry!). Comparisons are made between Joan Durbeyfield when she was young and Tess Durbeyfield in her youth. For Mrs Durbeyfield, Tess's main weapon in her quest to Trantridge is her face, her beauty (her sexual attractiveness), as it was for her in her youth. So, as far Joan Durbeyfield is concerned, Tess is simply doing what her mother would do in similar circumstances. In a short dip into Joan Durbeyfield's past, in chapter three, as she sits in Rolliver's Inn next to her husband, she thinks back to being courted by her husband, 'shutting her eyes to his defects of character, and regarding him only in his ideal presentation as lover' (III). This is precisely what Mrs Durbeyfield would have Tess do: ignore the defects in life. However, in a Thomas Hardy novel, defects are exaggerated – in the later novels to the point of immensity. And Hardy's protagonists can't ignore (or refuse to ignore) the many defects of life.

"IS IT LIKE THAT *REALLY,* TESS?"

Though *Tess of the d'Urbervilles* is an apparently 'realist' or 'naturalistic' novel, likened at the time to Emile Zola and George Eliot, there are many fantastical components in it: Tess's visions of Earth as a blighted star, for example, or her notion that trees have eyes, or imagining passing over the day of her death each year. There are more than a few scenes rendered spectrally or unusually: not just the sleep-walking, but scenes such as the dance at Chaseborough, for example, with the dancers moving in a 'luminous pillar of cloud' (X); the blackness at The Chase and Stonehenge; the unreality of technology (steam trains and threshing machines); the depiction of people as flies or specks on whiteness, and so on.

It is significant that Tess Durbeyfield is often asleep or in a dream-state at key points in the narrative: when Prince dies; before her rape; when Angel Clare first acknowledges her she talks of out-of-body experiences; at Angel's sleep-walking; when she comes back to the Herons; on the altar stone at Stonehenge, and so on. One critic suggested that Jude and Tess are often asleep or drowsy or drunk at key erotic moments (Jude's remarriage to Arabella, going to Aldbrickham with Arabella, Tess's rape), in order to excuse themselves from acknowledging their sexual desires. These are moments when erotic desire becomes 'unconscious', which suits the censorial late Victorian climate (R. Sumner,

1988, 159).

The writing of Tess Durbeyfield's rape reveals some key changes which Thomas Hardy made in later drafts:

Darkness & silence ruled everywhere around. Above them rose
                    in which were poised
the primeval yews & oaks of the Chase, & the gentle roosting
                    all about
birds in their last nap; & around them were the hopping rabbits & hares. But where was
Rose Mary's Tess's
Sue's *guardian angel; where was Providence? Perhaps, like that other god of*
            ironical
whom the Tishbite spoke, he was talking, or he was pursuing… (from folio 99; J. Laird, 73)

The early scenes of *Tess of the d'Urbervilles* are exquisite, but so apparently 'simple', it's a wonder that Thomas Hardy dared to write them. That is, the depictions – of Tess Durbeyfield and her sisterhood dancing in the field, John and Joan Durbeyfield in Rolliver's inn, Tess and Abraham on the cart, and so on – seem close to being so simple they're quaint and sentimental. All the time, though, Hardy's narrator invests the scenes with ironies and hints at future complications and sadnesses. It is Tess's personality, primarily, that embodies the reservations in the narrative. She is not convinced about her mother's enthusiasm for the relations at Trantridge, and is not impressed by her father's easy acceptance of being a noble d'Urberville. It is her father's revelling in the news, for example, that has him celebrating at Rolliver's inn and not being in a fit state to take the beehives to Casterbridge. Tess resents this debauchery. '"O my God! Go to a public-house to get up his strength!"' (III) It would be easy, in another context, to see Tess as the tiresome family conscience, someone a little stuck-up, who must be humoured but ignored (in fact, her mother does partly ignore Tess's high-mindedness).

It is also Jack Durbeyfield's clinging onto being 'Sir John' while doing nothing about it that encourages Tess Durbeyfield to go to Trantridge. 'His reasons for staying away were worse to Tess than her own objection to going.' (V) There are a number of reasons mooted why Tess does go to 'claim kin' – but the major reason is not that her mother wishes to have her find a husband; neither is it the ignoble task, as Durbeyfield sees it, of asking for help from well-off relatives; no, it is that Tess killed the horse and has to make good the crime. The narrator notes this burning coal in Tess's conscience a number of times. For example, when Alec d'Urberville charges over the hill in the gig, to pick up Tess, she hesitates. The narrator suggests that one of the things that decides her to step into Alec's dog cart, instead of taking the slow cart, is the sight of her family watching from a distance and 'possibly the thought that she had killed Prince' (VII).

These early scenes are very poignant, especially Tess Durbeyfield's leave-taking, which is seen from the viewpoint of the mother and her children. With an economy of words, the narrator suggests that Tess is moving out of her depth, and far out of the little enclosed world of Marlott and the Vale of Blackmore. The departure of Tess from her family takes place on a hill, at the boundary of the two regions, the Vale of Blackmore and the Trantridge region.

The leave-taking is depicted in a silent movie manner, mainly with visual descriptions, and no dialogue (except for the family: this renders Alec still a mystery). There is a separation already between the family and Tess Durbeyfield, who goes alone to meet the cart on the hill (Joan and the children opt to retreat). It's curious that there is no encounter between Alec d'Urberville and the family, who're some way off. Instead, they watch Tess climb aboard his dog cart (Joan had met Alec a few days beforehand). Later, when Alec returns in the novel, the meetings between Alec and Tess's family are again kept in the background. And then the narrator plays upon the tearful reactions of the children, who don't want Tess to leave: it's all cleverly orchestrated to create distance and emotion, with Thomas Hardy's customary flair for finding a visual manifestation for issues such as separation, distance, leaving home – and sadness and doubt.

The horseplay at the beginning of *Tess of the d'Urbervilles* expresses age-old heterosexual oppositions: Tess Durbeyfield has a male horse called Prince; Alec d'Urberville has a mare called Tib (a palindrome of 'bit'). The configuration of horses to humans doesn't need commentary – it underlines the sexual politics of the late Victorian novel. For example, Tess's horse is a tired old workhorse, essential for the family's survival; Alec's horse is primarily for his leisure. Alec's mare is significant, too, in chapter I. viii, in presaging the horse ride into The Chase and Tess's rape.

What happens is Alec intercepts Tess Durbeyfield on her journey to Trantridge and persuades her to ride with him. At this point, the sexual metaphor of 'riding' hardly needs pointing out. The erotic undercurrent is made clear when Alec is all for racing down the hills, while Tess holds back. Tib the mare becomes an equivalent for Tess's dubious situation, for Alec says she is a wild horse that must be mastered, and he has the power to do it (VIII). Further, Alec's mare has killed a man, and nearly killed Alec: the situation echoes Tess's own destiny in the novel. (D.H. Lawrence used horses in a similar manner in *Women In Love*, when he has Gerald ride his horse right up to a passing train, while Gudrun and Ursula watch in horror).

The horse ride to Trantridge, when the sexual relations between Tess and Alec d'Urberville begin (with the 'kiss of mastery'), looks forward to the rape scene: Tess's white muslin dress is blown 'to her very skin', and in the violation scene, Tess is seen as a 'white muslin figure' (XI). During the ride on the gig, the banks of the straight road look like a splitting stick (I. viii). The metaphor is vivid: it looks forward to the moment when Alec will penetrate Tess, splitting her body apart. The arguments on the Trantridge horse ride – whether or not to put her arm around him for safety, whether or not to ride with him – foreshadow the rape and her relations with Alec. Alec calls her a 'young witch', an 'artful hussy', and 'called her everything he could think of' (VIII).

Alec will always call Tess a whore, it is one of his many acts of violence against her.

Much of the argument in this scene stems from Alec d'Urberville's request for a kiss – in Victorian literature, as in much other art, a kiss is a synecdoche, standing in for sex. Tess Durbeyfield's reply is straightforward: '"[b]ut I don't want anybody to kiss me, sir!"' (VIII), and she begins to cry. Poor Tess: saying no is not enough, and Alec gives her 'the kiss of mastery' anyway (VIII). As with the rape, Tess tries to wipe off the mark of his kiss, just as Car Darch tries to wipe off the imprint of the sticky treacle off her back. Of the 'kiss of mastery', the narrator says that Tess tries to rub it away: '[s]he had, in fact, undone the kiss, as far as such a thing was physically possible' (VIII).

The kiss, of course, cannot be 'undone', even less can the rape be 'undone'. Tess Durbeyfield finds that being raped is an immense psychological scar that cannot be wiped away; and neither can being pregnant be 'undone'. For Tess, a huge social gulf opens between the person she was before Trantridge and the changed woman she is afterwards. Tess vows to return to her mother as she argues with Alec d'Urberville about riding with him. This is the point at which she could return, after being called a whore; but then her social conscience reminds her that she could not go back on such 'sentimental grounds' (VIII).

Tess's rape destroys the wholeness of the female body. It is an inscription which she can never erase. She tries, with her confession, to revenge her violation, but it doesn't work. The bitter irony of *Tess of the d'Urbervilles* is that even the murder of Alec does not erase the rape. How can it? The damage has already been done.

During Tess Durbeyfield's short time at The Slopes, Alec d'Urberville continues to insult her and stalk her. He follows her around, spies on her, even hiding behind a curtain at one point. Alec says that she offers him 'such temptation as never before fell to mortal man' (IX), making the first of many allusions in the novel to Adam, Eve and the Fall. Indeed, the narrator of *Tess* reminds the reader that, between 'Phase the First' and 'Phase the Second', after the rape, Tess Durbeyfield 'learnt that the serpent hisses where the sweet birds sing, and her views of life had been totally changed for her by the lesson' (XII). The masses of caged birds at Trantridge need no gloss as another equivalence of Tess's state – later on comparisons are made between Tess and caged animals, or animals on the run (as when she kills the pheasants out of mercy).

Critics have noted the use of symbols such as the colour red in *Tess of the d'Urbervilles* (T. Tanner, 1968). Far more wide-ranging, in a way, is the bird symbolism. Birds are everywhere in *Tess*: the caged birds at Trantridge; the herons at dawn at Talbothays; the pheasants Tess Durbeyfield kills; when Tess learns, after the rape, that 'the serpent hisses where the sweet birds sing'; the arctic birds at Flintcomb Ash ('gaunt spectral creatures with tragical eyes'), and so on.

Tess's induction into the excesses of the Chaseborough crowd, primarily dancing and alcohol (both of which she has known at Marlott), is described in one of Thomas Hardy's many moments of visual poignancy in *Tess of the d'Urbervilles*; she sees the dancers through a haze of candlelit dust (X). The fusty obscurity of the scene is an analogy not only of the confused, coughing, drunken state of the revellers, but of Tess's descent into increasingly ambiguous social situations. The narrator continually reminds the reader of the unreality of this particular night in September. He speaks of 'the ecstasy and the dream'; the 'soaring' thoughts of the party-goers in the 'sublime' and 'ardent' moonlight; the way their breathing, the night mist, the moonlight and 'the spirit of the scene' seemed 'to mingle with the spirit of wine' (108-113). You can see when Hardy's writing comes alive – and it does in his set-pieces, such as gatherings and parties.

It is ironic that one of the forces that persuades Tess Durbeyfield to climb onto Alec d'Urberville's horse again should be female sexual jealousy and resentment. Just as Tess's mother encouraged her to further her career via her sexual charms (her face or 'beauty'), so 'dark Car', the Queen of Spades, resents Tess's reserve which she sees as haughtiness. Again, Tess gets called a 'hussy', this time by Car Darch, who perceives Tess as a sexual rival. Tess does not see herself in this light at all, but in the unreality of the strange moonlit night, such subtleties are lost.

> *No sooner did the dark queen hear the soberer richer note of Tess among those of the other work-people than a long smouldering sense of rivalry inflamed her to madness. She sprang to her feet and closely faced the object of her dislike.*
> *'How darest th' laugh at me, hussy!' she cried.*
> *'I couldn't really help it when t'others did,' apologized Tess, still tittering.*

Car Darch's method of getting the treacle stain off her back is of course a grotesque parody of sex ('spinning horizontally on the herbage and dragging herself over it upon the elbows', X). Car Darch's wriggling again presages Tess's fate during the rape an hour or two later. When Alec d'Urberville arrives on the fight scene class relations are suddenly re-inforced, the revellers sober up and collect themselves to continue homeward. Tess's predicament is immense: '[a]t any other moment of her life she would have refused such proffered aid and company' (X). The act of accepting a ride with Alec a second time is seen as another of Tess's mistakes.

In the run-up to the rape, in the next chapter (I. XI), the narrator is firmly on Tess Durbeyfield's side (as usual). He describes how Tess has been up at five each day that week, has been on her feet all day, has waited for three hours without food or drink (XI). She is exhausted, at one of her many low points in the narrative. The narrator does allow Alec d'Urberville a certain integrity, in having Alec saying he feels 'responsible for [Tess's] safe conduct home' (XI). But this effort at nobility of Alec's comes after he has let the horse wander miles away, instead of taking Tess straight home. Alec's statements just before the rape imply that he did not intend to rape Tess, that he was merely enjoying riding on the horse with her.

But then the narrator turns his attention to Tess Durbeyfield as Alec d'Urberville returns: she is 'a pale nebulousness' in her white muslin dress (XI); she is absorbed back into the landscape, as far as the male gaze is concerned (K. Silverman, 1984); she is asleep and has been weeping, as if she has already guessed at Alec's real intention in bringing her to such an isolated spot (XI).

> 'Tess!' said d'Urberville.
> There was no answer. The obscurity was now so great that he could see absolutely nothing but a pale nebulousness at his feet, which represented the white muslin figure he had left upon the dead leaves. Everything else was blackness alike. D'Urberville stooped; and heard a gentle regular breathing. He knelt and bent lower, till her breath warmed his face, and in a moment his cheek was in contact with hers. She was sleeping soundly, and upon her eyelashes there lingered tears.

Then the narrator stresses Tess's virginity, using the classic metaphor of untrammelled white snow upon which is 'traced such a coarse pattern' (XI). Hardy's narrator depicts the scene as a man taking Tess's virginity against her will: in many feminists' views, this is defined as rape. The fact that it's rape is indisputable: the power relations between the two have already been emphasized by *Tess*'s narrator: the 'kiss of mastery', the power struggle with the mare Tib, the class superiority of the man, the man forcing fruit and flowers on Tess, and so on. The rape is a continuation of these male-female power relations.

"WHY DIDN'T YOU WARN ME?": THE RAPE OF TESS

Thomas Hardy's is a literature of loss. In *Tess of the d'Urbervilles*, everything fails: love, motherhood, ambition, folklore, custom, history, tradition, education, religion, and matriarchy. They all fail, or are lost. In Hardy's fiction, the most piquant loss is always loss of love. In *Jude the Obscure*, in Jude's first experience of erotic love, a Lacanian lack or void opens up inside him. 'She was not there now', the narrator says, so that 'a void was in his heart which nothing could fill' (I. vii). The irony is, with love comes the void, and the more one desires, the greater the hunger and the void becomes. Tess Durbeyfield, as the virgin Angel imagines her to be, i.e., Tess Durbeyfield as representation, 'makes good male lack through the fantasmatic restoration of phenomenal plenitude', commented Kaja Silverman in "History, Figuration and Female Subjectivity in *Tess of the d'Urbervilles*" (1984). Tess's loss is her innocence, her virginity and childhood. '"Why didn't you warn me?"' she asks her mother (XII). Parents are often blamed. But parents are not trained to be parents – they have to learn as much as children do. Except they don't.

> 'You ought to have been more careful if you didn't mean to get him to make you his wife!'
> 'O mother, my mother!' cried the agonized girl, turning passionately upon her parent as if her poor heart would break. 'How could I be expected to know? I was a child when I left this house four months ago. Why didn't you tell me there was danger in men-folk? Why didn't you warn me? Ladies know what to fend hands against, because they read novels that tell them of these tricks; but I never had the chance o' learning in that way, and you did not help me!'

Nature's law, in Thomas Hardy's ideology, is that parents have to push children out into the world to learn the hard way, by the thousand natural shocks. Hardy's point, which is his central argument, is that many of the most harmful knocks are not 'natural' at all, but made by humans. Nature's law is: live, and live now. There is no second thought, no delay. Tess Durbeyfield learns that most of the hard knocks come from people – even from herself (she was negligent and was partly responsible for the horse Prince's death).

Another way of stating the dilemma in *Tess of the d'Urbervilles* is 'the wrong man the woman, the wrong woman the man' (XI). As the rape is in progress, Thomas Hardy sidetracks with a philosophical discourse. Why is it, the narrator asks, that things go wrong? (XI). Tess later takes the rape in a fatalistic way, like the rural inhabitants: 'it happened'.

Is it rape in *Tess of the d'Urbervilles*? Obviously it is. Tess Durbeyfield is taken into pitch darkness, having not even kissed a man in a sexual manner, and is raped. This is utter horror. Not only is Tess raped, she becomes pregnant from this first sexual encounter. The rape makes manifest the patriarchal power of men, and masculinist society, in a brutal way. Tess has to learn – and quickly – that men have certain powers and privileges that must not be questioned. If one does question them, they'll shut you up – either men themselves, or their laws.

This is exactly what happens to Tess Durbeyfield. Like so many rape 'victims', she keeps quiet about it, naming neither the act nor the rapist. Tess doesn't confess, except to her mother, the one person she hoped would save her, or at least warn her.[9] For some feminists (often Anglo-American feminists), rape is a crime and a social institution which perpetrates patriarchal power. Marriage is sanctified rape in this second wave feminist view (one see this so clearly in Alec's later repossession of Tess, but also in Angel Clare's view of Tess: he calls her 'this little womanly thing… What I become, she must become. What I cannot be, she cannot be'" XXXIV). Both *Tess of the d'Urbervilles* and *Jude the Obscure* examine in detail the idea of marriage as legitimized rape.

American feminist Andrea Dworkin's outraged analysis of rape fits so well at times with the proto-feminist discourse of *Tess of the d'Urbervilles* and *Jude the Obscure*. For example, this passage from *Right-Wing Women*:

> *The propaganda stresses that intercourse can give a woman pleasure if she does it right: specially if she has the right attitude toward it and toward the man. The right attitude is to want it. The right attitude is to desire men because they engage in phallic penetration. The right attitude is to want intercourse because men want it. The right attitude is not to be selfish: especially about orgasm.* (1983, 81)

This describes the state of so many female characters in so many classic novels, by George Eliot or Charles Dickens or Jane Austen or Emily Brontë or Virginia Woolf, or Thomas Hardy. Regarding the heroines of classic novels – Clarissa, Tess Durbeyfield, Eustacia Vye, Catherine Earnshaw, Connie Chatterley – Andrea Dworkin's aggressive analyses of marriage in *Right-Wing Women* seems to describe an important part of women's sexual economy:

> *In marriage a man has the sexual right to his wife: he can fuck her at will by right of law. The law articulates and defends this right. The state articulates and defends this right. This means that the state defines the intimate uses of a woman's body in marriage; so that a man acts with the protection of the state when he fucks his wife, regardless of the degree of force surrounding or intrinsic to the act... But even where marital rape is illegal, the husband has at his disposal the ordinary means of sexual coercion, including threat of physical violence, punitive economic measures, sexual or verbal humiliation in private or in public, violence against inanimate objects, and threats against children. In other words, eliminating the legal sanctioning of rape does not in itself eliminate sexual coercion in marriage; but the continued legal sanctioning of rape underlines the coercive character and purpose of marriage. Marriage law is irrefutable proof that women are not equal to men.* (1983, 77-78)

Andrea Dworkin's concern, like Thomas Hardy's and other politically and socially committed writers, is oppression, and she has no doubts as to who is the oppressor, and what arguments the oppressor uses to further the cause of oppression:

> *The oppressor, the one who perpetrates the wrongs for his own pleasure or profit, is the master inventor of justification. He is the magician who, out of thin air, fabricates wondrous, imposing, seemingly irrefutable intellectual reasons which explain why one group must be degraded at the hands of another.* (1988, 198)

One (male) critic suggests that Tess Durbeyfield must have known something about what was happening to her at the first 'seduction' and at (more so) the second one. In this view, it demeans Tess to take away from her the responsibility for what was happening to her, even though her innocence (the first time) seems to excuse her (T. Winnifrith, 129).

A typical view of *Tess of the d'Urbervilles* is that the heroine is a sacrifice to appease society (J.J. Lecercle).[10] Tess Durbeyfield's function is also a scapegoat, someone who can be kicked now and then to satisfy the violence of others. Most of those others are male. Tess is the object of many males' fantasies and violence – Alec d'Urberville and Angel Clare mainly, but also the farmer, and the lecherous youth in the Chalk-Newton inn (XLII). Tess's mother, as well as men, sees Tess as a sexual object, an item of exchange with Alec d'Urberville. As Luce Irigaray writes, '[w]omen, signs, goods, currency, all pass from one man to another'.[11] Tess is passed around like a commodity with a high use-value (while she is sexually active – after that, older women are often abandoned). Tess's whole environment is thoroughly patriarchal. There are only a few enclaves of sisterhood, such as the milkmaids at Talbothays. Even then, though, the sisterhood's talk is mainly of Angel Clare and 'compulsory heterosexuality' (Adrienne Rich's term).

Tess Durbeyfield's predicament is terrible because, like so many beaten wives or abused people, 'she had no counsellor' (XXXIII). She has no one to confide in, as with characters such as Bathsheba Everdene, Eustacia Vye, Grace Melbury and Elizabeth-Jane. She is alone. Even the potentially powerful Talbothays sisterhood doesn't help her with her main problem. Tess has to learn about the pain of loneliness. 'But nobody did come, because nobody does', as the narrator of *Jude the Obscure* says (I. iv). Tess has to learn self-sufficiency.

Even so, after the rape, she goes back to work for her parents (something Alec d'Urberville and Angel Clare do not do). The life view in *Tess of the d'Urbervilles* is very narrow: the people in the rural regions think of love and labour, gossip and marriage, and little else. Tess Durbeyfield seems to be different from others with her perception of the stars, or the eternal sunrises. She cannot, though, escape the immense patriarchal pressures around her: to work, to conform, to marry, to have a family. And the pursuit of marriage becomes work in Thomas Hardy's fictional world. These may be social lies – the merits of labour and marriage – but all Hardy's protagonists have to wrestle with them.

Tess Durbeyfield, as a scapegoat, is subject to male projection, where men project onto women their faults and weaknesses. Feminists call this 'satanism' or 'demonization'. Whatever goes wrong, it must be the fault of women – hence Conservative politicians in the 1990s in Britain singling out young unmarried mothers as scroungers.[12] How could men, with their high ideals and desensitized personalities, be the 'guilty' ones? Tess takes upon herself the guilt. This is the obscenity of the novel, Thomas Hardy's 'offensive truth'.

Angel Clare re-inforces Tess Durbeyfield's guilt when he rejects her after the confession scene. He prefers a literary, mythical Tess; not a flesh and blood woman, but a Goddess, a literary creation. Via her confession, Tess forces Angel to confront her actual body, and to delete his spiritualized image of her: for Angel, Tess's body can 'incite more than one allegorization, thus putting both the validity and the uniqueness of his reading into question'.[13] Tess as Woman as image or text ('tex').

The problem is that men sexualize and fetishize everything – not just women. Both Alec d'Urberville and Angel Clare see Tess Durbeyfield in sexual terms, first and foremost. Their fetishized vision of Tess controls most of their attitudes towards her and their actions. Alec sees Tess as a pleasure ground in which he can satisfy his lust. Later on, Alec calls Tess a whore in numerous ways. Angel views Tess in similarly fetishized, erotic terms. Angel cannot handle her rape: it forces him to confront face-on her sexuality, and his sexualization of her. Rape is affirmed in patriarchal society, according to second wave feminists. Tess's problem is therefore society's problem: she has to speak the unspeakable. She has to say 'I have been raped'. But no one wants to hear it, or can hear it. Worse, Tess cannot say it: she is continually silenced. She has to tell Angel 'you, Angel, and society, condemn me. And you are all wrong'.

As Hélène Cixous writes:

> *Women should break out of the snare of silence. They should not be conned into accepting a domain which is the margin or the harem.* (E. Marks, 251)

For Wayne Anderson in "The Rhetoric of Silence in Hardy's Fiction", silence is central to Thomas Hardy's fiction: he claims that the rhetoric of Hardy's fiction is fundamentally 'a rhetoric of silence' (1985, 54). Sometimes Tess Durbeyfield is seen grappling with clichés, such as the one that Alec d'Urberville suggests: that women mean yes, sexually, when they say no. Tess's task is partly to reclaim language and the ability to express oneself (A. Poole, 342). Even when Tess does speak, she is ignored. Sometimes her silence indicates guilt and the suppression of her past; at other times it indicates resentment, eroticism or dumb subordination (H, 21).

One critic relates Tess Durbeyfield's predicament to the tension between desire and language in Julia Kristeva's philosophy.[14] There are key moments when forthright statements are required, but not made. For example, when Arabella returns from Oz in *Jude the Obscure*, and asks Jude what they ought to do, Jude drinks and lets Arabella lead him to a bout of sex in Aldbrickham, instead of making for an immediate divorce. One strong word about divorce might save him – because the very next day, Sue marries Phillotson. Similarly, the narrative of *Tess of the d'Urbervilles* is crying out for Tess to tell Angel Clare about her former life, before their relationship becomes too far advanced, but she doesn't.

TALBOTHAYS, THE SEMIOTIC REALM

Tess of the d'Urbervilles gets into its stride at the start of 'Phase the Third': 'The Rally' (155ff). Here the Hardy narrator begins a long and exalted description of Hardy's own homeland, the Vale of Great Dairies. This part of the planet is lovingly, erotically depicted. The prose defines a new stage in Tess Durbeyfield's life, a state of rebirth (one of the many that Tess undertakes). As the narrator puts it,

> *women do as a rule live through such humiliations, and regain their spirits, and again look about them with an interested eye.* (XVI)

The description of Talbothays is typical Thomas Hardy prose, with its lyrical, painterly long shots, its evocations of religion and paganism and the use of sound (the calls of the people bringing the cows home).

> *It was intrinsically different from the Vale of Little Dairies, Blackmoor Vale, which, save during her disastrous sojourn at Trantridge, she had exclusively known till now. The world was drawn to a larger pattern here. The enclosures numbered fifty acres instead of ten, the farmsteads were more extended, the groups of cattle formed tribes hereabout; there only families. These myriads of cows stretching under her eyes from the far east to the far west outnumbered any she had ever seen at one glance before. The green lea was speckled as thickly with them as a canvas by Van Alsloot or Sallaert with burghers. The ripe hue of the red and dun kine absorbed the evening sunlight, which the white-coated animals returned to the eye in rays almost dazzling, even at the distant elevation on which she stood.*
>
> *The bird's-eye perspective before her was not so luxuriantly beautiful, perhaps, as that other one which she knew so well; yet it was more cheering. It lacked the intensely blue atmosphere of the rival vale, and its heavy soils and scents; the new air was clear, bracing, ethereal. The river itself, which nourished the grass and cows of these renowned dairies, flowed not like the streams in Blackmoor. Those were slow, silent, often turbid; flowing over beds of mud into which the incautious wader might sink and vanish unawares. The Froom waters were clear as the pure River of Life shown to the Evangelist, rapid as the shadow of a cloud, with pebbly shallows that prattled to the sky all day long. There the water-flower was the lily; the crowfoot here.* (XVI)

When he comes to the Angel-Tess romance, Hardy's narrator takes his time. Arabella's romance with Jude is done in a couple of short chapters in *Jude the Obscure*, but Hardy gives himself the luxury of slowing down the pace at Talbothays. Angel, however, is as persistent and as intrusive as Alec, though not as obviously so. One strong word from Tess would flatten Angel (he's far weaker than Alec as a suitor), but she lets him court her. She is always silenced and shy in their meetings; he is pushy, but justifies his desire with Christian teaching. He resolves, for example, 'never to kiss her until he had obtained her promise' (XXIX). But he gives into impulse and kisses her, in an erotic moment, when Tess has just risen from sleep. These are probably the most erotic incidents in Hardy's work.

Even while he indulges in evoking an erotic reverie for the lovers, Thomas Hardy's narrator in *Tess of the d'Urbervilles* does not forget the themes of industry, marriage, family, history and economics. Alec d'Urberville, too, though not a part of the Talbothays sequence, is recalled to the reader's attention by the elder Clare speaking of dealing with the 'lax young cynic' (XXVII). Referring to Alec at this point is a typical novelistic device which reminds the reader of Alec and Tess's rape and her difficult life, which is by no means forgotten in the time of her new romance with Angel Clare. Citing Alec in the Talbothays sequence is like introducing the Devil into the paradisal time of the lovers, who are like a new Adam and Eve. Indeed, Alec appears as Satan later on, and Angel becomes the new Adam with Tess's sister as the new Eve.

The scene where Tess Durbeyfield hears Angel Clare's harp music and moves through the lush vegetation is one that critics have often discussed. All critics have noted the highly charged eroticism of the scene, with its 'damp and rank and juicy grass', its fabulous colours and scents, and the way nature covers Tess with 'thistle-milk and slug-slime'.

> The outskirt of the garden in which Tess found herself had been left

uncultivated for some years, and was now damp and rank with juicy grass which sent up mists of pollen at a touch; and with tall blooming weeds emitting offensive smells – weeds whose red and yellow and purple hues formed a polychrome as dazzling as that of cultivated flowers. She went stealthily as a cat through this profusion of growth, gathering cuckoo-spittle on her skirts, cracking snails that were underfoot, staining her hands with thistle-milk and slug-slime, and rubbing off upon her naked arms sticky blights which, though snow-white on the apple-tree trunks, made madder stains on her skin; thus she drew quite near to Clare, still unobserved of him. (XIX)

Feminists have noted that Tess's experience here is of 'transcendental ecstasy', a 'plateau of sexual ecstasy', of 'orgasmic dilation', as Rosemarie Morgan puts it in *Women and Sexuality in the Novels of Thomas Hardy* (88).

Indeed, the elements of female fluids and *jouissance* in this piece or writing are very pronounced. While patriarchal critics emphasize the stench of death in this pungent scene, feminist critics see it as one of the times of ecstasy for Tess in the novel: Angel's Orphic music is not the cause of Tess's ecstasy, but rather the trigger. Tess's *jouissance* goes far beyond Angel's. Female sexual liquids permeate not only the garden scene, but the whole novel – not only the many references to blood, but also to milk (Talbothays is seen as a Biblical land of milk and honey), to tears, dew on flowers (roses), and the juice of fruit (strawberries). The liquid metaphors and images point to a feminine, maternal space, the site of Julia Kristeva's semiotic, imaginary realm, a pre-œdipal space before the Law of the Father and the entry into the symbolic order.[15] It is this fluid, semiotic maternal space of bliss that lies utopically (and nostalgically)[16] behind the struggle and suffering of the 1891 novel.

In *Gender Trouble: Feminism and the Subversion of Identity*, Judith Butler writes of Julia Kristeva's semiotic mode:

Although the semiotic is a possibility of language that escapes the paternal law, it remains inevitably within or, indeed, beneath the territory of that law. Hence, poetic language and the pleasures of maternity constitute local displacements of the paternal law, temporary subversions which finally submit to that against which they initially rebel. (1990, 103)

One can look at the trajectories of Thomas Hardy's characters and see their rebellion as simply a temporary subversion of patriarchal norms (Eustacia Vye, Sue Bridehead, Tess Durbeyfield). Sue and Tess, in particular, painfully 'finally submit to that against which they initially rebel'.

Tess Durbeyfield being likened (by Angel Clare and the narrator) to figures such as Eve, the Magdalene and the Madonna is potentially controversial. Tess being compared to Artemis, Daphne or Diana, the virgin huntress figures, is understandable. In those Classical mythic types, the woman is the virgin of the woods pursued by lusty males. Likening Tess to Eve, however, is more problematic: it occurs in two outdoor, landscape scenes: with Angel at dawn, and with Alec in her garden at Marlott. In the first scene, Angel is Adam, and Tess appears to be Eve in her incarnation as a fecund Goddess figure.[17]

In the second scene, with Adam-Angel gone, Alec d'Urberville's appearance as the Devil, the phallic serpent in the garden, is inevitable. Here Tess Durbeyfield becomes the Eve who is instrumental in the Fall of humankind. ('Hardy exploits the story of the Fall without accepting the idea of sin' [David Lodge, 1966]). The virgin becomes a whore – Alec calls her a whore, and likens her to the whore of Babylon. To Angel's eyes she's the virgin, to Alec the whore, but to neither is she the mother type, the Virgin Mary. Tess as mother lasts barely a chapter, and does not feature as a relationship with any of the four men in her life (Alec, Angel, Mr Clare and John Durbeyfield). As the Virgin Mary, Tess is seen in an idealized pastoral setting, lavishing what is seen as excessive affection on her child. Julia Kristeva's notion of the pre-œdipal mother relates to Tess's strange period of motherhood. 'Her love hovers between a dangerous fusional overwhelming of the child (the phallic mother of psychosis) and abandonment' (Elizabeth Grosz, 1992, 199).

During the baptism scene, Tess Durbeyfield becomes exalted,

appearing as a saint, burning with religion. Thus, by the age of eighteen, she has moved from virgin to 'kept woman' (= used sexually, = whore), to mother, to saint, to being a kind of widow, mourning her child. In this state, as the sexual woman without children or a husband, the mythic figure of Mary Magdalene is appropriate (as far as the narrator of *Tess of the d'Urbervilles* is concerned, in terms of the story and themes). As the Magdalene, Tess is the 'holy whore', the 'sacred prostitute', who is not integrated into society as mothers or wives are, but who nevertheless always exists in relation to (as a function of) patriarchal Christianity. The comparison in the early morning scene between Tess and Mary Magdalene evokes a particular moment in the Christian story, where Christ has risen but remains untouchable. The *Noli me tangere* scene was depicted famously by Titian, among other Renaissance painters, and Thomas Hardy's dawn scene clearly echoes the misty blue light seen in Italian Renaissance art. This meeting between Jesus and the Magdalene impressed D.H. Lawrence, and became the starting-point for his last fiction, *The Escaped Cock* (a.k.a. *The Man Who Died*).

On the cart, delivering the milk, Tess Durbeyfield has a chance to confess to Angel Clare, an ideal opportunity. But Angel silences her, and does the talking for her. Tell me your 'precious history', he say patronizingly; '"I was born at so and so, Anno Domini"' (XXX). Tess gives up going for the major confession, and tells him instead that she is a d'Urberville. At this point, she could just as easily tell him all, it seems. But no. She's held back; Angel, too, is caught up in himself, in his love for her. He stills regards her as a child '"[y]ou are a child to me, Tess"'). He does not see that something serious is wrenching Tess apart as she weeps so violently after agreeing to marry him 'that it seemed to rend her' (XXX).

During their courtship, the narrator makes the erotic nature of Tess Durbeyfield's experience explicit. Tess's voice becomes decidedly orgasmic as she walks with Angel Clare in the countryside around Talbothays; the narrator speaks of her

impulsive speeches, ecstasized to fragments... the spasmodic catch in her remarks, broken into syllable by the lappings of her heart. (XXXI).

This fragmented, ecstatic outpouring, which expresses much more than the individual words, recalls the *écriture féminine* of French feminism, in particular Hélène Cixous' notion of the *jouissance* of women's speech, and also Julia Kristeva's theory of fluidity and disruption, the semiotic realm (H, 19). The narrator says that Tess's laugh at this time of bliss was 'unlike anything else in nature'. The word 'laugh' does not appear much in *Tess of the d'Urbervilles,* or in Thomas Hardy's fiction as a whole (or you don't think of Hardy's characters laughing much!). Here, Tess's laugh of ecstasy recalls Cixous' notion of the subversive laugh of women which disrupts patriarchy, which Cixous relates to the Medusa (in her famous 1975 essay "The Laugh of the Medusa"):

I, too, overflow; my desires have invented new desires, my body knows unheard-of songs. Time and again I, too, have felt so full of luminous torrents that I could burst... (E. Marks, 246).

Thomas Hardy later made Tess Durbeyfield more modest: in an earlier version of the manuscript, when Angel embraces Tess she 'panted in her impressionability and burst into a succession of ecstatic sobs'. This was later changed to: 'she sank upon him in her momentary joy, with something very like an ecstatic cry' (J. Laird, 128).

The wedding day of Tess Durbeyfield and Angel Clare is critical, as all weddings days are in Thomas Hardy's fiction. It is at this time that Tess and Angel must demonstrate what they are made of, not by what they do, but in their inner identity. Angel is the one who fails at this crisis time. He falls back on the double standard of patriarchy, where what is OK for the man (here, to break promises), is not OK for the woman. It is OK for men to sleep around, to have, as Angel calls it, 'eight-and-forty hours...

dissipation with a stranger', but not for women to have sexual relations before marriage (XXXIV).

There is much to discuss at this point in the 1891 story, and the honeymoon scene is packed with dialogue. Angel Clare begins by patronizing Tess Durbeyfield, calling her 'this little womanly thing' (ib.). Here, though, it is clearly Angel who is the 'little boyish thing'. Tess is still trying to sympathize and empathize with Angel: she considers him her double when he says he too has something to confess (ib.). He proves not to be her double or equal. Tess forgives Angel's pre-meditated sex with a stranger, while he cannot forgive her being raped. While it's OK for the man to fool around with women, in a deliberate, conscious manner, it is not OK for the woman to be raped against her will. Tess turns into the fallen woman here, Eve, the temptress who brings down her ideal mate. Angel excuses his 'eight-and-forty hours dissipation with a stranger', even though, in terms of his Pauline Christianity, it is condemned. Tess's rape, meanwhile, which ought to be pitied and forgiven, or whatever it is Angel Clare does in his Anglicized Middle Eastern religion, is suppressed. Tess has to learn to 'lie or die', as Andrea Dworkin puts it.[18] At this point, where Tess is silenced by Angel, she is also silenced by the novel: there is a break between 'Phase the Fourth', 'The Consequence', and 'Phase the Fifth', 'The Woman Pays'. Just when Tess begins to tell her story, there are blank pages.

THE GAPS IN THE TEXT

The blank pages between each Phase in *Tess of the d'Urbervilles* are critical, occurring during her rape, and her confession. Thomas Hardy did not put them there for no reason. The first break, between the first two Phases, looks like this:

> *As Tess's own people down in those retreats are never tired of saying among each other in their fatalistic way: 'It was to be.' There lay the pity of it. An immeasurable social chasm was to divide our heroine's personality thereafter from that previous self of hers who stepped from her mother's door to try her fortune at Trantridge poultry-farm.*
>
> End Of Phase The First
> --------
> *Phase the Second*
>
> *Maiden No More*
>
> XII
>
> *The basket was heavy and the bundle was large, but she lugged them along like a person who did not find her especial burden in material things. Occasionally she stopped to rest in a mechanical way by some gate or post; and then, giving the baggage another hitch upon her full round arm, went steadily on again.*

The break seems reasonably straightforward: Thomas Hardy's narrator has laid the framework for the narrative, and the titles of the two Phases – 'The Maiden' and 'Maiden No More' – seem to explain what has occurred in this first break. What may be in dispute is how much the event was a 'seduction' or a 'rape'. If one goes back over the 'Phase the First', one can put forward arguments for rape or seduction or whatever. For most feminists, though, Tess Durbeyfield is raped, and the break in the text serves to illuminate the event by its very omission. Hardy made it clearer in subsequent editions of *Tess of the d'Urbervilles* that force was used in the 'seduction' scene. He added the words which depicted Alec d'Urberville leaning down to Tess's face and finding tears. Afterwards, one of the field-women, in another addition to the original, mentions that '"[a] little more than persuading had to do wi' the coming o't, I reckon"' (XIV; J. Laird, 176). The reader has already seen Alec forcing Tess to accept a strawberry from Alec, a symbolically weighted moment which offers an equivalent for the rape, like Prince's death (see A. Brick, 1962, 118). For some critics, the gaps between the Phases hint at Hardy pre-censoring the narrative so that adverse opinions of Tess cannot be formed.[19]

For other critics, the gaps indicate how Tess Durbeyfield's sexuality evades being described by the narrative voice (J. Bayley, 189; P. Boumelha, 1982, 126-7). One can see how Tess is deliberately silenced by the narrator in the gap which occurs at her confession, but the other gaps offer different complications in the novel. For example, the first gap not only stands in for Tess's rape, it also enables Hardy's narrator to gloss over the details of her time with Alec d'Urberville. Presumably Tess was something like a 'kept mistress' for Alec at this time. The page break enables Hardy's narrator to simply sum up these few weeks - in which Tess may've slept with Alec a number of times - as a daze for Tess ('"[m]y eyes were dazed by you for a little, and that was all"' XII).

Another break in the narrative of *Tess of the d'Urbervilles* occurs between chapter XIII and XIV, which's Tess Durbeyfield's pregnancy. One can see how the description of Tess's pregnancy and childbirth would have not been possible in the serial of *Tess of the d'Urbervilles* in *Graphic* magazine, and not permissable in contemporary 1890s novels. However, this leap of months between chapters XIII and XIV misses out a hugely important experience in Tess's life. Instead, she is seen in a pose which echoes both the woman as worker and woman as mother, when she suckles her baby in an image redolent of thousands of *Virgin Mary With Child* paintings. The moments of crisis, of sex and death, are marginalized by the narrator.

The break between the second and third Phases is not as

significant as the others. The break between the third and fourth Phases ('The Rally' and 'The Consequence') turns on an erotic moment, the kiss between Angel Clare and Tess Durbeyfield. The erotic nature of this break is echoed again, between the fifth Phase ('The Woman Pays') and the sixth ('The Convert'), when Tess sees Alec d'Urberville again after years. The narrative between these Phases (3rd and 4th, 5th and 6th) remains pretty much continuous. Between the fourth and fifth Phase comes Tess's confession, discussed elsewhere, but a break between Phases that is over-shadowed by the two earlier important breaks occurs between the sixth Phase, 'The Convert', and the ironically titled 'Phase the Seventh: Fulfilment'. This gap depicts Tess's second, fatal fall, her return to Alec d'Urberville.

Much of 'Phase the Sixth: The Convert' depicts Alec d'Urberville's re-seduction of Tess Durbeyfield. As before, Alec appears as a persistent personality who will not be put off taking Tess for himself again. What Thomas Hardy's narrator declines to depict, as before, is the actual moment in which this act of repossession occurs. Again, Hardy's narrator leads up to the reclamation carefully, describing in detail Tess's family's ignominious journey to Kingsbere. Marian and Izz are seen for the last time in the novel, on the journey. The last time Tess is seen directly by the reader, so to speak, before Angel sees her at the Sandbourne hotel, is in Kingsbere church. Here occurs the last of Alec's unsubtle joke appearances, as a knightly d'Urberville atop a tomb.

Thomas Hardy's narrator does not depict exactly how Tess Durbeyfield agrees to leave her family and go with Alec d'Urberville to Sandbourne. The page break neatly excuses him from describing this critical moment. The reader is abandoned again, and has to supply the crucial details. For this is an *immense* change of direction for Tess: to have kept away from him for so long, then to give in and go to him. It's amazing, really. Does she 'have' to go? No. Is she 'forced' to? No. *Must* she go? No. Does she desire Alec? Better to say, does she desire love, to be loved? Yes. Angel recognizes what a passionate person she is ('for the first time Clare learnt what an impassioned woman's kisses were like', XXX).

The way the scene is played between Tess and Alec in Kingsbere Church indicates how they will get on in their second time together: he jokes with her, while she sits next to the d'Urberville vaults and wishes she was with the dead. Alec makes a joke about the d'Urberville ancestry which has a distinctly bawdy overtone: '"[t]he little finger of the sham d'Urberville can do more for you than the whole dynasty underneath"' (LII). In Shakespearean drama Alec's 'little finger' would take on a phallic gloss. Again, sex is aligned with economics: the way out Alec offers Tess always has both – no money from him without sex.

How much Tess Durbeyfield herself is to 'blame' for what happens to her is indeed the heart of the novel. The reader has already seen, in the strawberry sequence, that Tess partly consciously accepts what Alec d'Urberville offers her, and as the strawberry scene looks directly forward to the rape scene, Tess can be seen as being partly complicit in her catastrophe.

The narrator emphasizes Tess Durbeyfield's submissiveness, and many (male) critics have also seen Tess's passivity as her defining characteristic. Her 'passivity' is needed by the narrator in order to 'excuse' her from what happens to her. Whether it was rape or not, then, is crucial, because it reverberates throughout the 1891 novel. If it wasn't rape, then Tess's act of murder is wildly out of place. Alec, in short, does not 'deserve' such a fate, and such a drastic action is unnecessary. Even if Alec had raped her, Tess's act of murder is unforgivable in a so-called 'liberal', 'democratic' society. Tess's first act of 'revenge' for her rape, her confession to Angel Clare, backfires dramatically. In the second act of 'revenge', she makes sure it'll work, by stabbing Alec herself.

If Tess Durbeyfield is not raped, but seduced, and is complicit in the act, then it's not clear what her motives are when she stays with Alec d'Urberville for the following few weeks. Even if she is raped, she stays far longer than one would expect her to, bearing in mind her character, and how she acts in the rest of the novel. The point is that *Tess of the d'Urbervilles* does not present a simple black and white case; this is why it is such a rich work. It would be too easy and obvious if Tess was raped and Alec was a total villain (the way a Hollywood movie would write the script). It is precisely in those grey areas, on the margins between sex, desire, fear and need, that the novel is most interesting.

The narrator of *Tess of the d'Urbervilles* is ambivalent about the rape, which's partly what creates the confusions. Seen as having been 'mastered' by Alec d'Urberville, the act is seen as rape for Tess Durbeyfield; but the narrator enfolds Tess with desire, so that 'insofar as priority is given to the narrator's erotic gratification at the re-emergence of Tess as image, Alec's action will assume the status of a seduction', commented Kaja Silverman (1984).

Can a country maiden really be so 'innocent' of such things as sexual intercourse? Thomas Hardy's narrator would have the reader believe so. However, this is not Tess Durbeyfield's 'purity'. Tess takes in the strawberry half-willingly, and later possibly takes Alec d'Urberville into her body half-willingly. However, if the difference between seduction and rape is a question of degree, there is a world of difference between taking a strawberry and being raped, bearing a bastard child, being a single mother, seeing the child die and baptizing it. After eating the strawberry, Tess takes others, and goes about in a 'half-pleased, half-reluctant state'. This is also her emotional state when she is in a 'daze' during the few weeks with Alec – not really enjoying herself, certainly not 'happy', but reluctant to leave because of the material comforts. *Tess*'s narrator is unsure about Tess's sexuality: is she a sensual, erotic woman, or, as Angel Clare idealizes her, a fresh, pure, virginal woman?

"ONCE VICTIM, ALWAYS VICTIM – THAT'S THE LAW": TESS AS BODY AND TEXT

Just after she's been raped Tess Durbeyfield meets the religious texts man. Sure the scene is hardly subtle – Tess being confronted by the hypocrisy of Christian dogma: 'THY, DAMNATION, SLUMBERETH, NOT' and 'THOU, SHALT, NOT, COMMIT, ADULTERY'. This is sledgehammer storytelling, and Thomas Hardy knows it. It is another example of showing that, in Christianity, 'the letter killeth', which became central to the anti-religion polemic of *Tess*'s follow-up, *Jude the Obscure*. *Tess of the d'Urbervilles* explores and parodies the terrain of language and power (C. Thompson, 1983).

At this point in *Tess of the d'Urbervilles*, the social condemnation of Tess Durbeyfield's behaviour implied in these dogmatic sayings from Judæo-Christianity is straightforward. What is more interesting about the scene is that Tess is being hounded by society directly. As the six week episode with Alec d'Urberville is glossed over in the blank pages, what the reader sees is Tess going from being a 'maiden' to being a 'maiden no more' and having the conversation with Alec on her departure. A paragraph later, and the Biblical text man is with her. Soon they're having a theological discussion in the early Sunday morning in October (as you do). Just as Tess's mental landscape is 'blighted' by her rape, so the sign painter blights the countryside with his religious texts (C. Thompson, 1983). One man 'inscribes' his will and desire on her body, another man 'writes' his morality on the body of the Earth.

> '*Do you believe what you paint?*' *she asked in low tones.*
> '*Believe that tex? Do I believe in my own existence!*'
> '*But,*' *said she tremulously,* '*suppose your sin was not of your own seeking?*'
> *He shook his head.*
> '*I cannot split hairs on that burning query,*' *he said.* '*I have walked hundreds of miles this past summer, painting these texes on every wall, gate, and stile the length and breadth of this district. I leave their*

> application to the hearts of the people who read 'em.'
> 'I think they are horrible,' said Tess. 'Crushing! killing!'

Curiously, Thomas Hardy's narrator has the text writer refer to each saying as 'tex', not 'text'. It seems as if Hardy's narrator is deliberately drawing attention to the affinities between 'tex' and 'sex' (as well as 'Tess' – see below). A number of meanings may cluster around this emphasis. It's Tess's sex that is the pivot of much of the tragedy, or point, or theme, of the late Victorian novel. The narrative explores the nexus Tess-tex-sex (and 'Wessex', in the term coined by a critic 'Wes-sexuality'). The two things, sex and text, are of course seen as a continuity in deconstruction and post-Derridan philosophy. Critics speak of the 'sexuality of the text' (Roland Barthes' *jouissance*), but also of the 'textuality of sex' (Jacques Derrida, Paul de Man, J. Hillis Miller, and Julia Kristeva).

The 'sexuality' or *jouissance* of Thomas Hardy's texts is strident, and needs no explanation – humanist Hardy critics since the first Hardy reviews have been extolling it. The 'textuality of sex', though, and other postmodern and cultural theory notions, have only been addressed by a few Hardy critics (Margaret Higonnet, Elizabeth Langland, Peter Widdowson, John Goode and others). Tess as 'sex' has been discussed by feminist critics of Hardy, in particular the relations between sex and gender, the relations between being female, femininity and feminism. This is as expected from second wave feminism. Far less common are the studies of Tess as 'text'.

By calling the (religious) text a 'tex', the affinity is made by the narrator not only between 'tex' and 'sex' but also between 'text' and 'Tess'. Tess Durbeyfield herself is indeed the 'text' of the novel, the surface upon which each character 'writes' their own version of Tess. Her mother 'writes' her as a beauty who might materially enrich the family – Joan Durbeyfield literally acts as a fashion designer, dressing Tess up and standing back to admire her handiwork. Angel Clare 'writes' Tess as a virginal, pure, poetic country maid.

Tess as the 'tex' of the novel is a text to be followed closely, or ignored, a 'tex'/ Tess to be exalted but not read closely (by Angel Clare), to be loved for her surface beauty but ignored/ silenced (by Alec d'Urberville). As Helena Michie notes in *The Flesh Made Word: Female Figures and Women's Bodies*, Tess is a 'text to be read, interpreted, and edited by her two lovers' (112f). Both suitors see the surface Tess as a blemishless 'text' upon which they 'write' their own fantasies and projections. For Alec, Tess is a nebulous whiteness at his feet, passively waiting for him to make his mark of phallic lust upon her. For Angel Tess-tex is equally clad in virginal white, for he never shakes off that first sight of Tess in her white smock at the club-walking. As the epitome of 'virgin territory' for Angel, Tess must be as pure as an unwritten piece of blank paper, upon which he can inscribe his dreams. When he finds that someone has written over the virginal Tess-'tex', it's no wonder that Angel recoils in horror. Instead of purity he finds dirt, the white body has been blackened, and Tess's purity for Angel becomes abjected, in the Kristevan model.

As Julia Kristeva says of abjection, in her book *Powers of Horror: An Essay on Abjection,* it is the mud in Narcissus' pool, just what Narcissus would *not* like to find when he gazes erotically at himself. Kristevan abjection is what is neither inside nor outside, what is 'quite close but... cannot be assimilated. It beseeches, worries, and fascinates desire', is neither object nor subject, it destroys unity (1982, 1-15).

Julia Kristeva sees the artist's project as the purifying of abjection. This is what Angel Clare has to do, but his religion does not equip him for such a task. Abjection lies behind the history of religions: the abject is simultaneously the 'land of oblivion' and that 'veiled infinity', the moment 'when revelation bursts forth' (ib., 9). The abject is the borderland of ambiguity, a total subjectivity. Ironically, it is *jouissance* that

> *alone causes the abject to exist as such. One does not know it, one does not*

desire it, one joys in it [on en jouit]. *Violently and painfully. A passion.* (ib., 9)

The abject, though, is not an object, not something that can be named, not something assimilable, not something definable.

The abject is not the Other, nor is it otherness; it is not, either, the subject's correlative. The only quality that the abject has is that it is opposed to the 'I', the subject. The abject worries and seduces desire; yet it cannot be assimilated, so desire rejects it. Even so, there is an impetus or spasm, a leap that is made 'towards an elsewhere as tempting as it is condemned.' (ib., 1)

The different means of purifying the abject becomes the history of religions in Julia Kristeva's view in *Powers of Horror* (1982, 17). For the monotheic religions, abjection persists as taboo or exclusion, associated with defilement and pollution. When the abject encounters Christianity it becomes 'a threatening otherness – but always nameable, always totalizeable' (ib., 17). Out of the encounter with the sacred, the abject is written by the artist: art continues the work that religion does, and art will continue, when religion finally dies, to perform this catharsis. Kristeva writes:

> *In a world in which the Other has collapsed, the æsthetic task – a descent into the foundations of the symbolic construct – amounts to retracting the fragile limits of the speaking being, closest to its dawn, to the bottomless "primacy" constituted by primal repression. Through that experience, which is nevertheless managed by the Other, "subject" and "object" push each other away, confront each other, collapse, and start again – inseparable, contaminated, condemned, at the boundary of what is assimilable, thinkable. Great modern literature unfolds over that terrain: Dostoyevsky, Lautréamont, Proust, Artaud, Kafka, Céline.* (1982, 18)

One can add Thomas Hardy to that list.

Julia Kristeva's abject has a Lacanian subtext: it relates to Jacques Lacan's lack and *objet a*: '[t]he abject is the violence of mourning for an "object" that has always already been lost.' (ib., 15) This is Angel Clare's problem, and also Tess Durbeyfield's – it is also the problem of every Hardy lover. All Hardy's lovers, from Gabriel Oak to Sue Bridehead, are in a state of Kristevan abjection.

"THE WOMAN PAYS"

Tess Durbeyfield's debasement later on in *Tess of the d'Urbervilles* is as nothing, in a way, compared with her self-humiliation at Angel's feet. It is disgusting to see Tessfield collapsing at Angel Clare's feet and begging for forgiveness. The fault lies not entirely with Angel: Tess too is compounded by patriarchal lies and taboos. For the narrator, Angel is the weaker character: '[h]e looked upon her as a species of impostor; a guilty woman in the guise of an innocent one' (XXXV). Yet Tess's very body and presence makes the unspeakable – the rape – visible and unavoidable. While all those around her wish her to sweep it under the carpet, Tess's living presence makes the taboo painfully visible. She becomes a blot that must be eradicated. Her (sexually defiled) presence is too disruptive. In the end, society does get rid of it.

'The woman pays' – the men in the 1890s novel have the weight and authority of patriarchy and Christianity behind them. God cannot be wrong (he was a man), so it is the Devil, and the Devil is… a woman, as pop songs tell us. Tess Durbeyfield's presence, her wounded body, uncovers a secret that society wishes to keep hidden: that violence and inhumanity exists, and that it is often perpetrated by males. Not only violence, but the trade in women is exposed. As Luce Irigaray comments in *Ce sexe qui n'en est pas un*, 'woman is traditionally use-value for man, exchange-value among men. Merchandise, then'.[20]

This happens in Thomas Hardy's fiction: Tess Durbeyfield is 'traded' between Angel Clare and Alec d'Urberville, and is 'possessed' by both. Alec 'possesses' Tess physically, sexually, and Angel 'possesses' her sexually too, though by not sleeping with her. His possession works by a negation of eroticism, which, in the Christian way, still upholds the sexual status quo of patriarchal powergaming. Angel emphasizes her virginity, which reinforces the sexual status quo, which men dictate, and Alec emphasizes her eroticism, which also reinforces the status quo. Tess is seen as both virgin and whore by her men, much as the Goddess Aphrodite was both whore and virgin, and in Christianity there is the double aspect of the Mother of God: the virginal Mary and the prostitute Mary Magdalene. In other words, Alec screws Tess and possesses her, Angel doesn't screw Tess but still possesses her.

The trade or exchange in women in Thomas Hardy's fiction shows 'how fatal it can be to confuse a body with a sign': many of Hardy's male characters mistake their created image of a woman for the real woman (Angel with Tess, Boldwood with Bathsheba in *Far From the Madding Crowd*, Jude with Sue in *Jude the Obscure*, Dick with Fancy in *Under the Greenwood Tree*, and so on). The site of this fierce sexual, economic and ideological exchange is the female body, which in Hardy's *œuvre* is 'most conspicuously exchanged, inscribed, gazed at, deciphered, imitated, substituted for an ultimately replaced by something else' (Elisabeth Bronfen).[21] Tess Durbeyfield herself is full of noble principles and acts. She cares for other people, such as her father and mother, Izz, Retty and Marion; she is acutely conscious of Angel's reaction to her confession. She goes even further, suggesting her suicide. Tess is willing to go the whole way, and to sacrifice herself for love, the highest moral act in a truly Christian society. The problem is partly that Angel cannot do the same; he cannot put his arms around her and embrace her wholly. He recoils. He holds back from total surrender. The woman is more like the male ideal, Christ, than the man.

Men in *Tess of the d'Urbervilles* hold back, keeping something distant. Angel Clare doesn't realize Tess Durbeyfield's deep love for him. It takes sex to convince him of her passion – when she embraces him on the cart with 'an impassioned woman's kisses' (XXX). Tess cannot stop herself telling the truth, as she sees it. Her mother berates her for what she sees as a weakness in Tess's character: '"you little fool"'. Tess agrees, but says she could not blind Angel, it would have been a sin. '"But you sinned enough to marry him first!"' retorts her mother (XXXVIII). Yet Tess is not the only character to speak honestly at a crisis point: Izz does the same when Angel asks if she loves him more than Tess: '"[b]ecause nobody could love 'ee more than Tess did!"' (XL).

There is something in Tess Durbeyfield that Alec d'Urberville and Angel Clare do not see – her 'very self' (XXXV). Tess says '"I thought, Angel, that you loved me – me, my very self"'. Alas, no, he does not see her very self.

> 'I thought, Angel, that you loved me – me, my very self! If it is I you do love, O how can it be that you look and speak so? It frightens me! Having begun to love you, I love you for ever – in all changes, in all disgraces, because you are yourself. I ask no more. Then how can you, O my own husband, stop loving me?'

Tess Durbeyfield's sexually wounded presence exacerbates the ideological negation of women. *Tess of the d'Urbervilles* is a patriarchal text, despite its proto-feminism: Thomas Hardy was prevented by censorship from describing experiences such as pregnancy. Even mentioning pregnancy, let alone depicting it, was censored in Victorian times.[22] The feminism in *Tess of the d'Urbervilles* always makes concessions to the patriarchal, masculinist cultural climate of the late Victorian era. Hardy wanted to go further, depict even more harsh realities, but could not within the magazine market. Today, a hundred-plus years later, there are still many things that cannot be shown – even things as harmless and everyday as an erection. A scene such as the killing of the live pig in *Jude the Obscure* could not be shown on film or TV these days. Blasting away people, in Hollywood movies such as *Avatar*, *Die Hard* and *Rambo*, is acceptable, but not the killing of an innocent animal (even though people eat animals in their millions).

In *Tess of the d'Urbervilles* Alec d'Urberville keeps pushing, as men keep pushing. This is certainly seen in the behaviour of self-confident, socially-able men in Hardy's fiction, such as Edred Fitzpiers, Alec d'Urberville and Captain Troy: they embody the colonizing, territorial, phallic tendency described by feminists such as Luce Irigaray. Forbidden to speak for so long, Tess finally does speak: but her act of speaking destroys Angel's delicate constitution. There are few places where Tess is allowed to speak: the second is her letter to Angel; her third act of passionate speaking – to Alec, in her anger after meeting Angel in Sandbourne – goes unheeded. It is one of Tess's most passionate speeches:

> *'And then my dear, dear husband came home to me... and I did not know it!... And you had used your cruel persuasion upon me... you did not stop using it – no – you did not stop! My little sisters and brothers and my mother's needs – they were the things you moved me by... and you said my husband would never come back – never; and you taunted me, and said what a simpleton I was to expect him!... And at last I believed you and gave way!... And then he came back! Now he is gone. Gone a second time, and I have lost him now for ever... and he will not love me the littlest bit ever any more – only hate me!... O yes, I have lost him now – again because of – you!' In writhing, with her head on the chair, she turned her face towards the door, and Mrs Brooks could see the pain upon it; and that her lips were bleeding from the clench of her teeth upon them, and that the long lashes of her closed eyes stuck in wet tags to her cheeks. She continued: 'And he is dying – he looks as if he is dying!... And my sin will kill him and not kill me!... O, you have torn my life all to pieces... made me be what I prayed you in pity not to make me be again!... My own true husband will never, never – O God – I can't bear this! – I cannot!'* (LVI)

It is then (and very quickly) that Tess Durbeyfield decides to express herself in a different way: to kill. 'Culture, at least patriarchal culture,' Luce Irigaray contends in *Thinking the*

Difference: For a Peaceful Revolution, 'would prohibit then the return to *red blood,* and even sex' (107). In Irigaray's reading of patriarchy, society suppresses real life, with its painful blood mysteries. Instead there are pseudo-feminine blood mysteries, such as the Mass and Eucharist of Catholicism. Or, in patriarchal mythology, a heroic blood-letting, such as war, which appropriates women's mysteries such as menstruation in a distinctly violent and masculine way.

When women take up such aggressive ideological positions, masculinist society becomes very unsettled. Women hitting back at their male partners is still seen as unusual and as news in the early 21st century because it disrupts patriarchal norms. Focussing on women cutting off their husband's penises or murdering them covertly admits that women-beating is the norm. Men beating women is not seen as news or out-of-the-ordinary in Western patriarchal society. Viewed from a mainly Anglo-American feminist perspective, *Tess of the d'Urbervilles* records the suppression of red blood, feminine sex and wildness. The use of 'virile force' by men, as Marguerite Duras notes, reinforces the 'silence of women'.[23] In the end, Tess sees no alternative than to use men's means, the ones that have been used against her, against them. 'Rape plays a role in every form of sexual exploitation and abuse', insists Andrea Dworkiin in *Heartbreak*:

> *Rape happens everywhere and it happens all the time and to females of all ages. Rape is inescapable for women. The act, the attempt, the threat – the three dynamics of a rape culture – touch 100 percent of us.* (144)

Tess's fourth act of speaking is when she tells Angel Clare she has killed Alec d'Urberville:

> *I have done it... He had come between us and ruined us, and now he can never do it anymore. I never loved him at all, Angel, as I loved you... Why did you go away – why did you – when I loved you so? ...I could not bear the loss of you any longer – you don't know how entirely I was unable to bear your not loving me! Say you do now, dear, dear husband; say you do, now I have killed him!* (LVII)

Again, as with Alec not listening to Tess Durbeyfield before she killed him, this speech goes partially unheeded by Angel Clare. It requires Angel to say one of those odd Hardyan lines to ascertain the reality of the situation: '"What, bodily? Is he dead?"' Of course Alec must be *bodily* dead, for Tess has been bodily murdered throughout the novel. Only Alec's 'bodily' death satisfies the requirements of the sexual tragedy.

※

In the middle of *Tess of the d'Urbervilles,* during the confession scene, Thomas Hardy employs the age-old metaphor of fire: the honeymoon fire in the room dies down to ashes.[24] This is also the dark, cold lowpoint of the year, New Year's Day, in the bleak Mid-Winter. Hardy does not stop the novel at this point, though: as with his other novels, the failed marriage is but the beginning of a long descent. Tess plods on, like a Beckettian character. Even at Flintcomb Ash, during Tess's backbreaking sojourn, there is the possibility that everything will turn out all right – or at least not tragically. 'So the two forces were at work here as everywhere,' the narrator ponders: 'the inherent will to enjoy, and the circumstantial will against enjoyment.' (XLIII)

The next crisis point for Tess Durbeyfield is where she fails to make contact with Angel's parents. This scene – with the long, starlit walk along icy roads and the humiliation of Tess's boots being found by do-gooder Mercy Chant, Angel's one-time intended spouse – is typical Hardy. It contrasts erotic desire and spiritual yearning with harsh reality (cold, poverty, hunger) and social humiliation. Tess's failure to reach Angel's parents, the narrator notes, is 'the greatest misfortune of her life' (XLIV). This would assume that Angel's parents would have helped Tess finally, as their son had failed to do. Perhaps not, though: the elder Clare, in particular, had a fierce and dogmatic Christianity, which may have prevented him from accepting Tess and her plight. Indeed, because of his influence on his sons, Angel Clare's father's rigid religiosity is partly responsible for Angel's own social constraints. The narrator even underlines the relation between Angel and the Church by having him tell Tess '"I love the Church as one loves a parent"', thus echoing the relation between the Freudian ego and the super-ego, the Law of the Father. (But the Church, traditionally, is seen as feminine, as the 'bride' of Christ – the sheltering Mother Church. Angel makes this explicit when he adds '"I shall always have the warmest affection for her"' XVIII). When Mr and Mrs Clare do realize Tess's state and feel sympathy for her, it is her sin that ignites their compassion:

> *the tenderness towards Tess which her blood, her simplicity, even her poverty, had not engendered, was instantly excited by her sin.* (LIII)

Angel Clare's father's religiosity is described at length by the narrator when Angel breaks his Talbothays idyll to travel to his parents to speak to them about his marrying Tess Durbeyfield. The narrator emphasizes that the elder Clare's Apostolic, Conversionist and Evangelical views are seen as out of date by his contemporaries (can Christianity be 'out of date'? It's already 2,000 years-old). The narrator points to the extreme asceticism of Father Clare, likening his negative, 'renunciative philosophy' to Arthur Schopenhauer. Significantly, for the elder Clare the *New Testament* was 'less a Christiad than a Pauliad' (XXV). The teaching of St Paul lies behind much of Angel's idealism and asceticism, which's shown vividly in his promising not to kiss Tess Durbeyfield until she had pledged herself to him, and in his renunciation of her after her confession. The narrator makes it clear that daddy Clare would have been 'antipathetic in a high degree' to Angel's relationship with Tess (XXV). The narrator hardly needs to illustrate the difference between the two environments, sensual Talbothays and austere Emminster, by having the black puddings being given to the poor of the parish.

The overbearing Christian renunciation of the patriarch Clare is instrumental in helping to form Angel Clare's response to Tess Durbeyfield at the crucial time of the confession. The elder Clare is basically kind-hearted, however, as the narrator points out (XXV), while Angel has to learn such compassion over hard months in Brazil. The implication in the text is that Angel's father would not have turned away from Tess at the crucial moment, but would have confronted the dilemma, just as he kept persevering with Tess's seducer, Alec, when Alec berrated him.

In the discussion between Angel Clare and his father about Alec d'Urberville, the difference between son and father is made clear: Angel wishes his father would not get involved with such people – Angel's tendency, as he shows in the confession scene, is to turn away. His father, though, simply gets on with the job of encouraging sinners to change their ways. The irony is that Angel's father is the father Tess Durbeyfield would like, ideally: a strong-willed, principled, ascetic man, as opposed to the harmless but relatively ineffective and drunken father she has. It may also be that Angel's father, of the three men (Alec, Angel and Clare), is the one more suited, in a way, to be Tess's husband. He at least, like her, has moral and social principles, and is not so concerned with pressing forward his ego and personality upon people, as Alec and Angel are.

Later on, around the time of Tess Durbeyfield's aborted mission to Emminster, the austerity of the Clares' religiosity is tempered, as they become increasingly concerned about their son in Brazil, and the marital estrangement of Angel and Tess. It is Angel's mother who finally elicits the real details about the break-up from Angel. But Mrs Clare's intervention transgresses the religious code of the household, and it is the elder Clare's patriarchal Christian stance which remains predominant.

There are differing degrees of pain and humiliation in Thomas Hardy's fictive world. To be poor and struggling is one thing, but to be pursued by a rapist is another. At times, Tess Durbeyfield does cry out against her stalker, goaded on by the smarmy, conniving man:

'Don't go on with it!' she cried passionately, as she turned away from him

> to a stile by the wayside, on which she bent herself. 'I can't believe in such sudden things! I feel indignant with you for talking to me like this, when you know – when you know what harm you've done me! You, and those like you, take your fill of pleasure on earth by making the life of such as me bitter and black with sorrow; and then it is a fine thing, when you have had enough of that, to think of securing your pleasure in heaven by becoming converted! Out upon such – I don't believe in you – I hate it!' (XLV)

One can applaud Tess Durbeyfield's moments of fighting back against Alec d'Urberville, but she is more alone than ever. In Thomas Hardy's world, there is no help, no advice, no safety net, no one to catch people when they fall. They just keep falling. It is too much to expect Angel Clare to help her – he is caught up in himself, fraught by Tess's disruptive revelation. When Tess admits she has been raped, she is defiled in Angel's view, and he does what many do when confronted with defiled people – he runs away.

The irony of Alec d'Urberville's 'conversion' to Xianity is massive, and perhaps the most unbelievable part of *Tess of the d'Urbervilles*. It is as difficult to take as the death of Jude Fawley's children in *Jude the Obscure*. It is, of course, Angel Clare's father who converts Alec to Pauline fervour. And it is Angel, through Tess Durbeyfield's words, who helps to convince Alec that he ought to shake off his religiosity. Similarly, and as ironically, it is Jude who introduces Sue Bridehead to his future love-rival, Phillotson. Angel, the morally righteous one, the would-be Cambridge priest (like Jude, and Thomas Hardy himself at one time, who considered taking up a role in the Church), goes off to Brazil to pursue the thoroughly secular life; meanwhile, Alec, the utterly profane sexual predator, turns spiritual. Both acts of Tess's suitors are heavily ironic, and in the circularity of the novel both men return to their former selves.

Alec d'Urberville's new religious mania is constantly referred to by the narrator as he re-seduces Tess Durbeyfield. The re-seduction becomes a religious as well as a sexual assault. Christianity is used (ironically) to justify lust. Like so many others,

Alec projects his lecherous desires onto the woman.25 Somehow, Alec gets away with his verbal attacks of Tess and his stalking of her. All of Alec's sickness gets loaded onto Tess at this point. Unable (or unwilling) to deal with his own dissatisfactions, he calls Tess a whore: '"[y]ou temptress, Tess; you dear damned witch of Babylon'" (XLVI). Alec's sickness simply reflects society's sickness – simply exaggerates Alec's villainy, making him an extreme version of a weak, violent, manipulative and dishonest man. Alec is all phallic power – he is the phallus at large, seeing, possessing, colonizing, exploiting. The narrator has the phallic aspect of Alec's character emphasized when Alec mentions going to Abbot's-Cernel, that is, Cerne Abbas in Dorset (XLV), where the Cerne Giant drawn in chalk on a hill has the biggest penis in Britain (thirty feet long). This part of *Tess of the d'Urbervilles* is perhaps the most 'unrealistic': the reappearance of Alec and his pursuit of Tess does have a mythic, allegorical flavour.

Alec d'Urberville may not be as villainous as a conventional reading of *Tess of the d'Urbervilles* might suggest. There is evidence, critics have pointed out, that he actually loved Tess Durbeyfield, and may even have loved her throughout the novel (unlike Angel Clare); he offers to help Tess when she first leaves him, and when her husband has deserted her; he buys things for her family; he feels angry when Tess is working for Farmer Groby and is treated badly by her employer; Tess may even 'use' him to a certain extent, though Alec expects something in return. If Alec is not all bad (and he can't be, or Tess would have had nothing to do with him at all); then his death becomes unnecessary. If Alec had loved Tess continuously through the novel, his death is vastly out of proportion with the emotions in the narrative.

While Alec d'Urberville does what he likes (though he is a slave to (his) lust), Tess Durbeyfield labours in the fields. She has responsibilities – to her family, her parents and friends, as Maggie Humm (1995, 38). The men do not have to look after anybody, they are socially mobile. Alec gives up wandering as a preacher and rides his horse again, taking up the leisurely life of the financially well-off. Alec is not all bad, of course: there are men much worse in their sadism than Alec. One imagines that Thomas Hardy, if not constrained by Victorian values in magazine publishing, would have gone much further in depicting Alec's depravity. For D.H. Lawrence, Alec may be Tess's true 'mate': '[n]o ordinary man could have betrayed Tess', Lorenzo reckons.[26] It was not so much Alec as the whole gender he was a part of that betrayed Tess. It was her ideals and hopes for life that were betrayed. It was not Alec who betrayed her, but all the people around her. Tess thought society was much better than that. She was also disappointed that a life could be ruined by rape and unmarried motherhood. Sex shouldn't be able to ruin people. Indeed, it doesn't ruin Tess: she gets up, dusts herself off, and carries on living.

Angel Clare is just as patronizing as Alec d'Urberville – he calls her 'child' and 'little thing'. Angel does not become violent with Tess Durbeyfield, like Alec, but he does hit someone in the inn who insults her. Tess is not exceptional, the narrator says, and Thomas Hardy says this in his writings about the novel. Tess wants what society wants (and pressurizes) her to want: a man, a husband, a heterosexual, domestic life full of work and children. The novel severely criticizes these demands of society, as feminists do, and how they are manifested in the individual. What Hardy despises is the social law that demands 'you must be married' and then says 'don't come to us if it goes wrong'.

Society demands participation – not only in marriage, but in being sexual. Even if one isn't married, one must have a sexual life. Feminists have noted that heteropatriarchy not only demands 'compulsory heterosexuality' (Adrienne Rich's phrase), but also compulsory sexuality. To negate sexuality, to be celibate or prefer not to deal with sexuality, is partly to be a non-person. Sexuality is such a large part of the construction of identity, in patriarchal societies, that people cannot understand it when others wish to subvert it. Thus, Alec cannot understand Tess not wanting to be in an erotic relationship with someone. Her husband absconding in Brazil, Tess simply wants to be left alone to get on with living. For Alec, this is madness, a waste of a life. There she is, with her soft body, which he must have.

Tess Durbeyfield regards Alec d'Urberville at times as her 'natural' husband – that is, as her true partner, sexually as well as socially. When she meets Angel in Sandbourne she says that the '"step back to him was not so great as it seems"', again emphasizing that she regarded her erotic relations with Alec as more fundamental, in the eyes of society, than her spiritual relationship with Angel. Angel too emphasizes the 'naturalness' of Alec being her husband: '"[h]ow can we live together while that man lives? – he being your husband in Nature, not I"' (XXXVI).

Both Angel Clare and Tess Durbeyfield emphasize the importance for themselves of sexual relations: Angel in his reaction to Tess's rape, and Tess in regarding her rapist as her 'natural' husband. Through Tess and Angel society expresses the widespread significance of sex. Alec d'Urberville also uses the 'natural' argument, but couches it in moralist language: '"has not a sense of what is morally right and proper any weight with you?"' he asks Tess as he tries to persuade her to marry him (XLVI). The term 'nature' is deployed with immense irony, of course.

J. Hillis Miller asked questions of *Tess of the d'Urbervilles* in *Fiction and Repetition,* such as, why is it that Tess is doomed to repeat the same event/s in her past and in the ancestral past, in her life, and other people's lives? (116). The continual questions of 'why?' that *Tess of the d'Urbervilles* raises at each point of crisis are the ones that readers ask of all Thomas Hardy's fiction. Why does Tess seem to be relatively immature or 'less shrewd and worldly-wise' than she might be expected to be? (Arnold Kettle asked in *Hardy the Novelist* (54). Why doesn't she know about men and sex, when she lives in a lively rural community in which people would presumably have spoken frankly about sex? Also, with her group of friends of the same age, sex and boys would have been topics of conversation, as they are in women's magazines such as *Shout, Mizz* and *Bliss* (and probably have been discussed between teenagers for at least 40,000 years). Why did Tess go to Trantridge, knowing what Alec's intentions probably were? Why didn't she try another job, and remain in Marlott? Why didn't she tell Angel about her past in another letter, when the first one was mislaid?

More questions: why didn't Angel Clare turn back to find Tess after Izz had told him she would have done anything for him? (wondered Roy Morrell in *Thomas Hardy: The Will and the Way*). He was 'within a featherweight's turn' of doing so. If Tess had told him of his sleepwalking, which she was on the point of doing, it might 'have prevented much misunderstanding and woe' (XXXVII). The night before, after he's been out wandering and wondering, Angel goes up to check on Tess. He turns to leave her bedroom, then turns back again, as if to enter her room (and also to enter her body – it's their honeymoon night). But he catches sight of the d'Urberville portrait, which unsettles him (XXXV). There he is, outside her bedroom, on his wedding night, knowing underneath he really loves her, and knowing that she adores him, yet he doesn't go in. Scared off by a painting! What (Christian) renunciation!

Many of these questions stem from Thomas Hardy's plots. Why the sudden passivity in characters? Why the unbelievable coincidences? Why the misunderstandings? Hardy's novels do not bear up to too much analysis in terms of plot, action and causality. In *Tess of the d'Urbervilles,* there are many moments when Hardy's plot stretches credibility. One is inclined to keep asking, as little Abraham does, '"[i]s it like that *really*, Tess?"' (I. iv)

> 'Did you say the stars were worlds, Tess?'
> 'Yes.'
> 'All like ours?'
> 'I don't know; but I think so. They sometimes seem to be like the apples on our stubbard-tree. Most of them splendid and sound – a few blighted.'
> 'Which do we live on – a splendid one or a blighted one?'

> '*A blighted one.*'
> "*'Tis very unlucky that we didn't pitch on a sound one, when there were so many more of 'em!*'
> '*Yes.*'
> '*Is it like that* really, *Tess?*' *said Abraham, turning to her much impressed, on reconsideration of this rare information. 'How would it have been if we had pitched on a sound one?*'

Many (male) critics find themselves a little exasperated at Miss Durbeyfield's occasional 'passivity', which's manifested in her emphasis on negation, death, and in the recurring Hardyan wish of never having been born. For these critics (T. Wright, I. Gregor, R. Morrell), Tess Durbeyfield's apparent 'passivity' becomes fatal: she lets things happen to her as much as making them happen. She seems to 'let' Alec d'Urberville and her mother manipulate her, dress her up, organize her life. Bert Hornback reckons in *The Metaphor of Chance: Vision and Technique in the Works of Thomas Hardy*, that 'Tess's tragic flaw is her seduction by Alec d'Urberville' (111). Her most catastrophic passivity may be when she lets Angel leave her. The narrator notes that with a little more effort in the right direction, she could make him stay with her. The reasons she doesn't are many, but her d'Urberville pride comes into it: it is partly this pride that prevents her for so long from contacting Angel's parents. Hardy criticism in its modernist, humanist, mid-20th century phase, tended to see Tess as a 'victim', a 'tragic victim'. Tess is complicit in the power relations between herself and her two suitors. To Alec she calls herself a victim and slave: '"[w]hip me, crush me... Once victim, always victim – that's the law!"' (XLVII); and to Angel she says '"I will obey like your wretched slave, even if it is to lie down and die"' (XXXV).

To continue our rewriting of *Tess of the d'Urbervilles* with more questions: why does she go back to Alec d'Urberville? She loves Angel Clare so much, she wants to be back with him so badly, as her letters demonstrate, so why does she return to Alec? The reasons and causes given in the text do not wholly explain it.

Reasons for her return in terms of the story might include: *(1)* feeling guilty about her family's homeless plight; *(2)* not seeing Angel for over a year – and Alec is there, before her, in the flesh, offering money, security, sensuality; *(3)* she has heard nothing from Angel; *(4)* Angel offered to take Izz Huett. One can conjure up many reasons.

Yet Tess Durbeyfield's previous time with Alec d'Urberville was awful – she knew she was blinded by him – a daze lasting a few weeks she calls it.[27] The death of her father comes at a key point, March 10, when Tess has gone to the extreme of yearning for Angel Clare's return and cannot seem to hope any longer. The father's death is another key cause in Tess's decline – it takes the house away from the family. Yet Jack Durbeyfield's death is hardly described in the text. It is a major character's death, the main one after Tess's death and her baby's death. Yet the funeral isn't even mentioned, and there are no mourning scenes, as one might expect from Hardy (he's never one to pass up a good funeral scene). Instead, Durbeyfield's death is a plot point, and *Tess*'s narrator moves on swiftly to the house-ridding. This event, of far less import, perhaps, than Jack's death, is depicted in full. Tess's father's death is quickly forgotten – strange that it is not spoken of between Tess and all the characters: her mother, her family, Alec or Angel when he returns.

Thomas Hardy's narrator accelerates the events in the last Phase of *Tess of the d'Urbervilles*, as if he has plotted it all out in detail, seeing how it would all fit together. Hardy said of *Jude the Obscure* that he always had the ending in mind as he wrote the book: it is the same with *Tess of the d'Urbervilles*. Tess Durbeyfield's death lurks underneath the text through the narrative. It is the fact, the scar, the reality that will never go away – and only Tess herself cannot see it (she passes over her death-day each year, not knowing which date it is). For Tess, her death is the ultimate blindspot. Yet, increasingly, in 'Phase the Seventh', Tess becomes more and more death-conscious.

Then there is the problem of her letters. They are superb,

especially the two-page love-letter, in which Tess Durbeyfield wrote to Angel Clare:

Angel, I live entirely for you. I love you too much to blame you for going away, and I know it was necessary you should find a farm. Do not think I shall say a word of sting or bitterness. Only come back to me. I am desolate without you, my darling, O, so desolate! ...How silly I was in my happiness when I thought I could trust you always to love me! I ought to have known that such as that was not for poor me. But I am sick at heart, not only for old times, but for the present. Think – think how it do hurt my heart not to see you ever – ever! Ah, if I could only make your dear heart ache one little minute of each day as mine does every day and all day long, it might lead you to show pity to your poor lonely one. (XLVIII)

In the poem 'Tess's Lament' her case is expressed in similar language:

And now he's gone; and now he's gone:...
　　　　　And now he's gone! (CP, 176)

Tess Durbeyfield moves from an oral to a written culture, from folk ways to civilization, from speech to *écriture*. *Tess of the d'Urbervilles* describes 'the masculinzation of Tess's voice and the feminization of Angel's' (H, 24). But why did Tess wait so long before writing to Angel in South America? Or, more correctly, why did Thomas Hardy's narrator wait so long before including Tess's letters in the text? Angel had been having a terrible time in Brazil for months, so one of Tess's passionate letters (which he cherishes when they do arrive), would probably have changed his mind. Returning sooner to Wessex, Angel may have been reunited with Tess. His return was only a few weeks too late, but that's plenty in Hardy's erotic world. '"Too late, too late!"' says Tess mournfully (LV).

'It is too late,' said she, her voice sounding hard through the room, her eyes shining unnaturally.
　'I did not think rightly of you – I did not see you as you were!' he continued to plead. 'I have learnt to since, dearest Tessy mine!'
　'Too late, too late!' she said, waving her hand in the impatience of a

person whose tortures cause every instant to seem an hour. 'Don't come close to me, Angel! No – you must not. Keep away.'

The meeting of Angel Clare and Tess Durbeyfield in the Sandbourne hotel is a dialogue of starts and stops, with inarticulacy constantly threatening to slip into uneasy silence. Tess keeps repeating 'too late', while Angel tries to make some sort of moves towards a love-reunion. Tess says she waited and waited, but Angel didn't return. Eventually, she explains to Angel that Alec d'Urberville has won her back, that he is upstairs, that she hates him. To this, Angel has no response. This is *the* decisive moment for Angel: does he take Tess by the hand and lead her gently but firmly away from her hateful life with Alec? Right there and then? No. He lapses into silence: 'he could not get on. Speech was as inexpressive as silence' (LV).

Tess Durbeyfield is not the only character to be silenced, then. But Angel Clare's sorrowful lapsing into an awkward silence is not the only unusual aspect of the scene – although it is odd that Angel was stuck for words, the Angel who was so articulate, who knew the names of the gods and goddesses of mythology, who knew about the finer points of theology – but Angel's insight that 'his original Tess had spiritually ceased to recognise the body before him as hers' (LV). This is a crushing view. It shows how Tess has allowed Alec to re-colonize her, to do with her as he wished. It indicates the extent of Tess's suffering, how she is letting Alec take any advantage of her body that he wishes. It is a version of the 'fanatic prostitution' of Sue Bridehead (in Jude's phrase) in *Jude the Obscure*. It shows just how bereft Tess's life has become, how spiritually (and socially) empty. This crucial insight of Angel's, though, is made after his visit. At the time he simply stands there; she leaves; then he finds himself outside: he too lacks any will.

It can be seen as another instance of Tess Durbeyfield's strange passivity, that she didn't write sooner to Angel Clare. And why, crucially, didn't Tess write to Angel's parents? As she is shy, it would have been far better, instead of walking all that way across half of South Wessex to Emminster, in her best clothes, if she had written to the elder Clare. One of her carefully crafted letters would probably have deeply affected Angel's father. Tess showed in her passionate letter to Angel that she could create marvellous prose (handcrafted by one of England's great novelists). If that wouldn't have suited Tess, she could have primed Angel's parents with a note stating her arrival on Sunday, before voyaging to Emminster. Just a note, saying she would call after lunch. So easy. Tess could also have done all the begging for money by letter. Two or three letters setting out her position, establishing a rapport with the elder Clare. In the ensuing charitable friendship, money or help of some sort would surely have been forthcoming from the Clare home. Very likely they would have offered to have her live in their house until Angel's return. After all, the Clares helped Alec, and Angel, so why not her? One visit would have done it. Failing that, why didn't Tess simply step aside when the people came out of the church, and wait, and then call on Clare? Or leave a note with a servant, saying she'd wait near the church, or leave a note at the house.

Perhaps the Clares could have done nothing for Tess Durbeyfield: but Angel could have: one note from him, saying he still cared for her (and would perhaps return to her), would have been enough to sustain her. It would have strengthened her resolve to withstand Alec d'Urberville. Also, it would have been physical evidence that he still cared for her. She could have shown Alec the letter at a pinch. Angel could have sent money, at least, if not via her mother then via his father. It is Angel hiding things from his parents that contributes towards the problems, as well as Tess withholding information from Angel. People are shy in the 1891 novel, rarely speaking their own minds. Tess's mother does not tell her about her secret plans for her daughter; similarly, Izz and Marian hold back from telling Angel about Tess. Both Tess and Angel loved each other, so what kept them apart? Angel did not need to spend such a long time in Brazil, from 3 weeks into January after they were married to his return the following mid-April. He could have stayed for six months, not fifteen months. Besides, Angel may well have given up on Tess after fifteen months away from her. It is in her nature to keep loving him for years, but not in his.

Why does Tess Durbeyfield have to kill Alec d'Urberville? She could simply have left him. He was still in bed. She could have walked out of the door with Angel Clare. She may have had a few belongings with her at the Sandbourne hotel, but nothing she would have minded leaving behind. Or she could have gone upstairs, dressed, said she was going out to buy something she needed, and left with Angel. On the way to Emminster, Tess would have been re-united with Angel, and his parents too would be reconciled with her and their son. They'd leave for a farm in the North of England. If Alec brought the case to court, he would probably lose, and anyway Tess could still leave him for Angel.

Instead there's the murder – again, significantly, not shown: Thomas Hardy's narrator is more concerned with the effect or impact of the murder, than the act itself. The murder means blood is spilt, and this is what is shown, coming through the ceiling. Significantly, language again plays a key role in the murder sequence: Alec calls Tess's beloved a 'foul name' and this is partly what drives her to murder him – literally, to shut him up. Similarly, when Jude Fawley is weak and seemingly incapable of sudden direct action, he leaps up to pin Arabella down when she calls his beloved Sue a hussy. Having been silenced herself, by a host of social, psychological and cultural factors, Tess finally manages to silence her pursuer – to have, as far as *she's* concerned, the last word. At the beginning of the novel, he forced the strawberry (phallic object) in her mouth, now she thrusts back the phallic object, the knife.

What would have been laudable would be if Angel Clare had confronted Alec d'Urberville in the hotel: if he had strode up the stairs, to fight over Tess Durbeyfield, much as Michael Henchard and Donald Farfrae fight over a woman in *The Mayor of*

Casterbridge. This would be the classic Hollywood scenario greatly desired by the audience in a 1940s Hollywood film of *Tess*.

Angel Clare's reaction at this crisis in the Sandbourne hotel – to walk away sadly – says it all about his character. It is up to Tess Durbeyfield to be the strong, decisive one. Just as Tess goes to Alec twice, so Angel abandons Tess twice (and Jude marries Arabella twice, and so on). The narrator says that Angel's love was 'doubtless ethereal to a fault, imaginative to impracticability', and suggests that personalities such as Angel perhaps prefer 'corporeal absence' to corporeal presence, because the absence of the body aids their idealization (XXXVI). One would have thought Angel would have learnt his lesson. But no. No confrontation for him. And no grabbing Tess by the hand and pulling her out of the hotel, along the road to the station, like the ending of the 1967 movie *The Graduate*. And then, after killing him, why does Tess lose her sense of will and direction? Why does she not seem bothered about running away with Angel?

During the short idyll in the empty house Thomas Hardy had originally written:

> *"All is trouble outside there; inside here content."*
> *He peeped outside also. It was quite true; within was affection, pity, error forgiven: outside was the inexorable.* (LVIII)

Thomas Hardy changed one word here in 1892: altering 'pity' to 'union'. The result – 'affection, union, error forgiven' – makes their brief time together more joyous.

※

The incestuous undercurrent in *Tess of the d'Urbervilles* is even more 'controversial' than the cousin configuration in *Jude the Obscure* (between Sue and Jude), for 'Liza-Lu is Tess's sister. The ending of *Tess of the d'Urbervilles*, though evoking a (at least for the moment) non-sexual relationship between Angel and 'Liza-Lu, transgresses the social and moral law. A man could not marry his sister-in-law at the time of the novel (1891). (The Deceased

Wife's Sister Act was passed in 1907). What saves the Angel-'Liza-Lu relationship from being seen as incestuous or controversial is the intense spiritualization at the end of *Tess of the d'Urbervilles*, where the future Adam and Eve are shown kneeling down and praying silently, motionlessly. (The Angel-'Liza-Lu relationship is very swiftly delineated: at Stonehenge, Tess urges Angel to consider marrying 'Liza-Lu, then, four pages later, she's dead and the novel's over).

The final sentence of the 1891 novel has much more power than the much-discussed 'President of the Immortals' phrase: '[a]s soon as they had strength they arose, joined hands again, and went on.' (LIX)

'A WHOLE SEX CONDENSED INTO ONE TYPICAL FORM'

Tess Durbeyfield is, as critics have noted, the centre of the novel.[28] Many (often masculinist) critics have spoken of Tess as a 'passive', 'simple' country woman or 'maid'.[29] Irving Howe is a typical (male) Thomas Hardy critic, and writes of *Tess of the d'Urbervilles* in a sexist manner.

> *For in* Tess *[Hardy] stakes everything on his sensuous apprehension of a young woman's life, a girl who is at once a simple milkmaid and an archetype of feminine strength. Nothing matters in the novel nearly so much as Tess herself.* (Norton *Tess*, 400)

Even though Irving Howe is sympathetic to Tess Durbeyfield, he refers to her as a 'simple milkmaid'. It is in these (un)subtle ways that masculinist criticism reveals its patronizing attitude towards female characters in literature. Thus, Tess is a 'simple milkmaid', just as Marty South is a 'simple girl', rather than a hard-working, acutely sensitive young woman. Indeed, it is

Angel Clare who is really the 'simple' character in *Tess of the d'Urbervilles*. It is Angel's blindness and ineffectuality that drives Tess to the ultimate waking-up act, murdering Alec d'Urberville.

Like must mix with like in Tom Hardy's fiction. Hardy's romances have an insistent materialistic undercurrent. This is most powerfully displayed in *Tess of the d'Urbervilles*. The Tess-Angel relationship embodies so well the clashes between the rural and the middle classes, between the values and *mœurs* of the country people and the bourgeoisie. Tess Durbeyfield literally embodies the agricultural world – physically, culturally and spiritually. She is portrayed by the narrator as sensuous, pure, close to nature, accepting the rigours of existence, dealing with the present. Angel Clare has a dry, distanced and impure kind of spirituality and religion. He is blind, and plays at farming. He does not see Tess fully, nor does he fully experience agriculture. His Christian religion sets up barriers – it is not as life-affirming as Tess's paganism. Hardy uses these two lovers to point out so many hypocrisies in society. In Tess and Angel he sets up the struggle between agriculture and industry, between paganism and Christianity, between a feminized culture of the land (of magic, superstition, nature, growth, labour, season and community), and a patriarchal culture of the machine (Christianity, science, control, and city-life).

Tess of the d'Urbervilles is probably the most accomplished example of Thomas Hardy's union of the concerns of class, labour, materialism, sexual politics and social status. *Tess of the d'Urbervilles* brilliantly exposes the hypocrisies found in the notions of inherited and earned rank, in labour and economy, in property and ownership. Hardy ruthlessly highlights the brutality inherent in these problematical areas of the human condition. Alec d'Urberville's gift to Tess Durbeyfield is sex and materialist wealth. He buys her disinherited family a horse; he gives Tess a kind of home in the Sandbourne hotel. Angel Clare gives her spirituality, but nothing materially. Alec, though a false aristocrat, is practical. Angel, more noble, is impractical. His Brazilian escapade goes terribly wrong. John Durbeyfield finds out he is a descendant of a titled and prestigious county family, but he is not able to do anything with this knowledge. Joan Durbeyfield is more practical. She sends Tess away, but also withholds important information from her daughter about sex and men's predatory nature.

Tess of the d'Urbervilles is not only a great novel of the tensions between nature, sexuality, character and spirituality, it also engages face-on the vicissitudes of class, labour, wealth, knowledge and economic politics. Thomas Hardy's Wessex is not only a world of nature, emotion, personality and the spirit of place (the Hardy of the romantic heritage novel, beloved of prestige television serializations), it is also a world of great social change, in which the ideological forces at work are altering rapidly. The working class figures – Marty, Oak, Tess, Jude – try to cling on to the old ways of earning a living. Tess and Marty carry on working in the way they have always done. But they are overtaken by a new group of controllers, who have new methods. The way that Tess and Jude try to earn a living is far below what they are capable of doing.

Tess Durbeyfield has her independence and nobility, but she pays dearly for it. Tess goes down to the bedrock of socio-economics. She is alone, she must eat to live, so she works. Her London education does not help her at all. Her solution is entirely practical. 'Social life is essentially practical', wrote Karl Marx (1942, 473). Thomas Hardy's novels operate in the Victorian worlds of cruel socio-politics, of Marx's philosophical materialism and revisionism, or extreme poverty and rapid change. 'The socio-political systems of the era did help to strengthen the domination of the bourgeoisie over the proletariat', wrote Vladimir Lenin (in ib., 57). There's no need for a Marxist analysis of *Tess of the d'Urbervilles*, because the novel is its own best analysis.

❦

Gender and received gender roles play an important part in the economic and socio-political aspects of Thomas Hardy's Wessexscape. It is true that the women in his novels are too often stereotypes – the possessive mother, the betrayed maid, the neurotic aristocrat, and so on. The role of working women in a patriarchal society is a central concern of Hardy's fiction. He knew that women could be cruelly underpaid (Per, 186).

In *Tess of the d'Urbervilles* he shows how a woman wanting to work on her own, outside of a domestic situation, will be the victim of all kinds of masculinist manipulation. Tess Durbeyfield is a prey to rape, hard labour, bad pay, patronizing male attitudes, patriarchal double-standards and an inadequate male-made justice system. Though one thinks of Hardy's age as archaic, poverty-stricken and quite different from our own, some things have not changed. Women still earn today on average 74% of what men earn. Poverty, disease, famine, slavery, prostitution and dictatorship are still at work in the contemporary world. These problems are far worse now than they were in Hardy's era, because the number of people suffering is millions and millions more.

"JUSTICE WAS DONE…': TESS'S END

Astonishingly, Tess Durbeyfield remains hopeful throughout the narrative. She will not be trodden into the soil of Wessex, even though she is 'soiled' by several men. The will to live drives Tess along, but it is also the will to pleasure, as the narrator notes during the Angel-Tess affair:

> *to snatch ripe pleasure before the iron teeth of pain could have time to shut upon her: that was what love counselled; and in almost a terror of ecstasy Tess divined that, despite her many months of lonely self-chastisement, wrestlings, communings, schemes to lead a future of austere isolation,*

love's counsel would prevail. (XXVIII)

Tess Durbeyfield is one of the great survivors of literature, even though she dies. One of the amazing things about *Tess of the d'Urbervilles* is that it involves the death of the heroine – after she has already been raped (J. Goode, 1988, 137). Yet *Tess of the d'Urbervilles* remains a life-affirming text. Despite the many mistakes, confusions, backtrackings and failures, and the narrator's sometimes gleeful dwelling on them, *Tess of the d'Urbervilles* is an inspiring text. Tess impresses because, as D.H. Lawrence writes, she 'never tries to alter or to change anybody... She respects utterly the other's right to be' (*Study*, 95).

Tess is not a 'feminine' text in the Hélène Cixous manner, nor does it articulate the Kristevan *chora* like *avant garde* modernist writing. *Tess* is not the expression, either, of the two lips speaking together of Luce Irigaray, nor is it the articulation of the female 'wild zone' of Elaine Showalter.

It is, however, a novel of rage and oppression which feminists such as Andrea Dworkin, Adrienne Rich, Alice Walker and Susan Griffin might applaud. Despite being a feminist or proto-feminist novel, *Tess of the d'Urbervilles* is popular with critics partly because it flatters and reflects their views. *Tess* has been popular with male critics because there is plenty in it that does not severely challenge their masculinist, patriarchal views and ideologies. If *Tess of the d'Urbervilles* were an openly radical feminist text, it would probably not have achieved its status as one of the most discussed books in literature. Very few aggressively feminist books become classics.

Tess of the d'Urbervilles is successful too because the reader is invited to identify wholly with the heroine, in the classic way of the Hollywood movie.[30] *Tess of the d'Urbervilles* is also successful because it does everything a good novel should do: it has a strong story and settings, powerfully rendered characters, important themes, and so on.

ILLUSTRATIONS

Illustrations of *Tess of the d'Urbervilles* in publishing, film and television.

Tess of the d'Urbervilles in illustrations:
Joseph Sydda, Tess In Dairyman Crick's Yard (above).
Hubert von Herkomer, 'There stood her mother, amid the group of children,
hanging over the washing tub', from Graphic magazine (below).

An early movie version of Tess (above).
'Tess's Seduction', one of E. Borough Johnson's
illustrations for the serialization in Graphic magazine
(below).

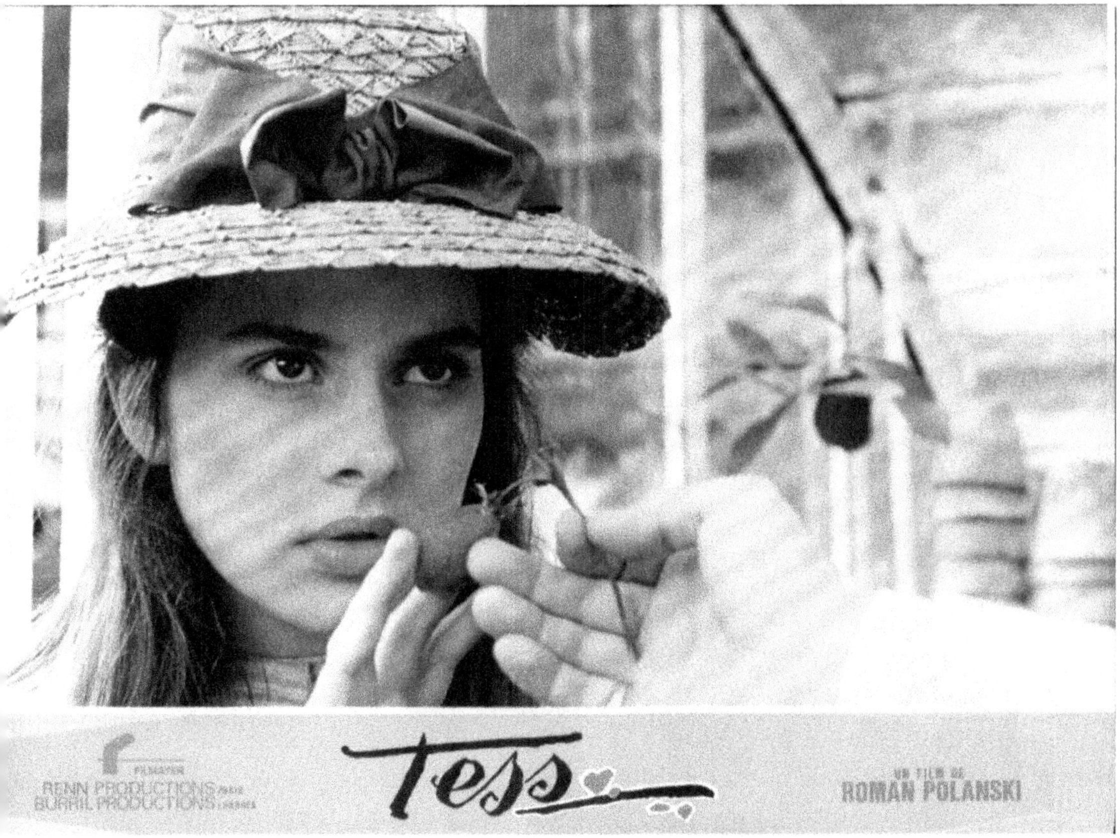
FILMAYER
RENN PRODUCTIONS PARIS
BURRIL PRODUCTIONS LONDRES
Tess
UN FILM DE
ROMAN POLANSKI

RENN PRODUCTIONS
PARIS
BURRIL PRODUCTIONS
LONDRES
FILMAYER
NASTASSIA
KINSKI
en
Tess
Un film de
ROMAN POLANSKI
NASTASSIA KINSKI · PETER FIRTH · LEIGH LAWSON
GUION DE GERARD BRACH · ROMAN POLANSKI · JOHN BROWNJOHN SEGUN LA NOVELA DE THOMAS HARDY
MUSICA PHILIPPE SARDE FOTOGRAFIA GEOFFREY UNSWORTH · B.S.C. GHISLAIN CLOQUET · ASC
DECORADOS PIERRE GUFFROY VESTUARIO ANTHONY POWELL PRODUCTOR EJECUTIVO PIERRE GRUNSTEIN
COPRODUCTOR TIMOTHY BURRILL PRODUCTOR ASOCIADO JEAN-PIERRE RASSAM DIRECTOR PRODUCCION PAUL MAIGRET
UNA PRODUCCION RENN PRODUCTIONS BURRILL PRODUCTIONS
SOCIETE FRANCAISE DE PRODUCTION (S.F.P.) RODADA EN PANAVISION®
PRODUCIDA POR Claude Berri

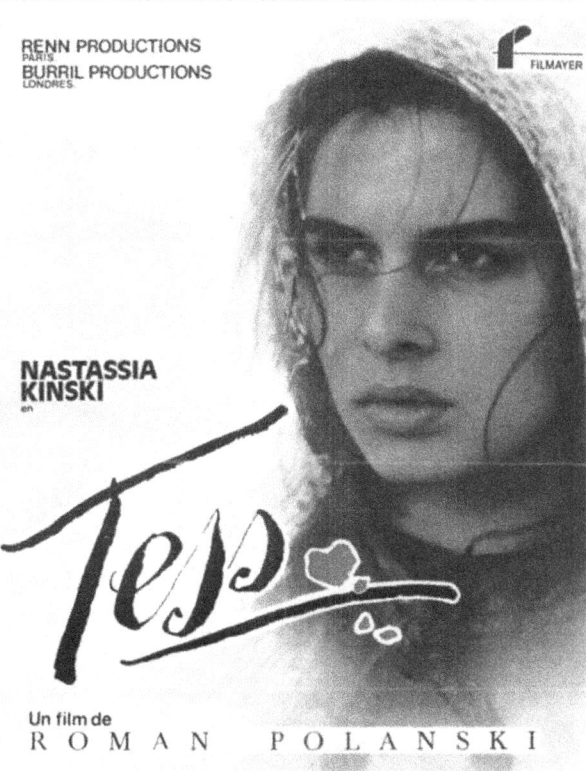

NOTES

1 Introductory

1. J. Hillis Miller: "Steven's Rock and Criticism as Cure, II", *Georgia Review*, 30, 1976.
2. Hélène Cixous: *Jours de l'an [First days of the year]*, 1990, in H. Cixous, 1994, 185.
3. F.R. Leavis: "Hardy the Poet", *Southern Review*, 1940; *The Great Tradition*, London, 1948.
4. Patricia Stubbs, for example, writes that Thomas Hardy is 'almost unique in the English nineteenth-century novel, in that he creates women who are sexually exciting' (1979, 65).

2 Thomas Hardy and Feminism

1. Peter Widdowson comments in his book on Hardy:

Hardy, as we have him, is so inscribed with the processes of the consumption and reproduction of his work in history that it is now, as it were, a palimpsest of the perceptions, evaluations, readings, re-readings, and re-writings of a particular literary and æsthetic – not to say national – tradition. (1989, 57)

2. Sarah Kozloff: "Narrative Theory", in R. Allen: *Channels of Discourse*, Methuen, 1987, 55.
3. Most Thomas Hardy criticism is distinctly patriarchal, it is 'based on a reading determined by a dominant gender ideology', and there's no doubting that this bias is masculine (George Wotton, 183).
4. Donald Hall, "Afterword", *Tess of the d'Urbervilles,* Signet, New York 1964, 424.
5. Judith Mitchell: "Hardy's Female Reader", in H, 178.
6. Robert Kiely: "The Menace of Solitude: The Politics and Aesthetics of Exclusion in *The Woodlanders*", in H, 188.
7. Luce Irigaray: "Sexual Difference", in T. Moi, 1987, 124.
8. Judith Halberstam: "F2M: The Making of Female Masculinity", in L. Doan, 1994, 212.

9. Sue Wilkinson & Celia Kitzinger; "Dire Straights?: Contemporary Rehabilitation of Heterosexuality", in G. Griffin, 1994, 84

10. Catherine MacKinnon: "Feminism, Marxism, Method, and the State: An Agenda for Theory", in N.O. Keohane, ed. *Feminist Theory: A Critique of Ideology*, Harvester, 1982.

11. Critics such as A.O. Cockshut remain adamant: '[t]he attempt to turn Hardy into a feminist is altogether vain' (*Man and Woman: Love in the Novel 1740-1940*, Collins, 1977, 129).

12. The sexual relations in Hardy's fiction, as in all fiction, occur within hetero-patriarchal ideology. As Elizabeth Grosz writes: '*All* sexual practices...are made possible and function within the constraints of heterosexism and phallocentrism', but these are not perfect, immutable systems, Grosz asserts, 'they are contradictory systems, fraught with complexities, ambiguities, and vulnerabilities that can and should be used to strategically discern significant sites of contestation' ("Refiguring Lesbian Desire", in L. Doan, 1994, 69).

Adrienne Rich, in "Compulsory Heterosexuality and Lesbian Existence", writes that 'gender inequality' also means 'the enforcement of heterosexuality for women as a means of assuring male right of physical, economical and emotional access' (1980).

13. Sherry B. Ortner: "Is female to male as nature is to culture?", in M. Rosaldo & L. Lamphere, eds. *Woman, Culture and Society*, Stanford University Press 1974.

14. Ann Rosalind Jones: "Writing the Body: L'Écriture féminine", in E. Showalter, 1986, 363.

15. L. Irigaray: *Ce sexe qui n'en est pas un*, Minuit, Paris 1977, 28-29.

16. Moira Gatens: "Power, Bodies and Difference", in T. Barrett, 1992, 134.

17. J. Kristeva: "La femme, ce n'est jamais ça", *Tel Quel*, Autumn 1974, in E. Marks, 135.

18. Hélène Cixous: "Sorties", in E. Marks, 95.

19. J. Kristeva: *About Chinese Women*, 63.

20. The phrases come from C. Schwichenberg: *The Madonna Connection: Representational Politics, Subcultural Identities and Cultural Theory*, Westview Press, Boulder, CO, 1993; R. Braidotti, *Patterns of Dissonance*, Polity, 1991; see J. Butler, 1990; S. Wilkinson in G. Griffin, 1994.

21. Becky Rosa sees monogamy as an ideology which society encourages women to conform to by using 'cultural products (the media), economic restraints (tax incentives, the high cost of single living), social factors (the provision of support and companionship, or social status and privilege) and by the notion that this is 'how it is', 'this is natural'' (1994, 107-8).

22. Christobel Mackenzie, 1993, 144.

23. John Kucich in H, 234; P. Stubbs, 1981, 58f; P. Boumelha, 1982, 48.

24. J. Kristeva: *Women's Time*, in *The Kristeva Reader*, 191.

25. Christian Metz, "The Imaginary Signifier", *Screen*, 16, 2, Summer 1975

26. L. Irigaray: "The poverty of psychoanalysis", *The Irigaray Reader*, 101.

27. Helena Michie makes this point in relation to Pierston in *The Well-Beloved*, in *The Flesh Made Word: Female Figures and Women's Bodies*, 112.

28. Luce Irigaray: *Speculum of the Other Woman*, 1985; see also: Dorothy Leland: "Lacanian psychoanalysis and French feminism: toward an adequate political psychology", *Hypatia*, 3, 3, Winter 1989, 81-103.

29. Elizabeth Grosz: "Refiguring Lesbian Desire", in L. Doan, 75.

30. R. Rilke, letter to Clara Rilke, 8 March 1907, in *Gesammalte Briefe 1892-1926*, Insel Verlag, Leipzig 1940, II, 279f.

31. J. Lacan, "The meaning of the phallus", 1988; Bernard Baas: "Le désir pur", *Ornicar?*, 83, 1987.

32. C. Jung: *The Development of Personality*, vol. 17, Routledge, 1954, 198; Marie-Louise von Franz: *The Psychological Meaning of Redemption Motifs in Fairy Tales*, Inner City Books, Toronto 1980, 39f.

33. Lady Jayne ad, *Clothes Show* magazine, December 1992.

34. See Laura Mulvey: "Visual pleasure and narrative cinema", *Screen*, 16, 3, 1975, 6-19.

35. Kristin Brady: "Textual Hysteria: Hardy's Narrator on Women", in H, 89.

36. Catherine King: "The Politics of Representation: A Democracy of the Gaze", in F. Bonner, 136. Luce Irigaray, "Women's Exile", in D. Cameron, 1990, 83; and Luce Irigaray, *Speculum*.

37. Dianne Fallon Sadoff: "Looking at Tess: The Female Figure in Two Narrative Media", in H, 151.

39. Emma Pérez: "Irigaray's Female Symbolic in the Making of Chicana Lesbian *Sitios y Lenguas (Sites and Discourses)*", in L. Doan, 108.

40. Hardy's letter to Alexander Macmillan, July 25, 1868, in M. Seymour-Smith, 1995, 85.

41. Sappho, in *Greek Lyric Poetry*, ed. W. Barnstone, Schocken Books, New York 1977, 4.

42. Stendhal, *De l'Amour*, Penguin 1975.

43. J. Kristeva: "In Praise of Love", in *Tales of Love*, 6.

44. Hélène Cixous: "Extreme Fidelity", in S. Sellers, 1988, and in H. Cixous, 1994, 132.

45. Kristin Brady: "Textual Hysteria: Hardy's Narrator on Women", in H, 94. In her essay "Refiguring Lesbian Desire", Elizabeth Grosz describes desire in post-Lacanian/ Hegelian terms which accords with desire in Hardy's fiction:

The only object desire can desire is an object that will not fill the lack or provide complete satisfaction. To provide desire with its object is to annihilate it. Desire desires to be desired. Thus, for Hegel, the only object that both satisfies desire yet perpetuates it is not an object but another desire... Desire is the movement of substitution that creates a series of equivalent objects to fill a primordial lack.

The mechanics of desire also have an economical dimension explored most fully in *Tess*. 'Now this notion of desire as an absence, lack, or hole, an abyss seeking to be engulfed, stuffed to satisfaction' continues Grosz,

is not only uniquely useful in capitalist models of acquisition, propriety, and ownership (seeing the object of desire on the model of the consumable commodity), but it also inherently sexualizes desire, coding is in terms of the prevailing characteristics attributed to the masculine/feminine opposition, presence and absence. Desire, like female sexuality itself, is insatiable, boundless, relentless, a gaping hole that cannot be filled or can only be temporarily filled; it suffers an inherent dependence on its object(s), a fundamental incompletion without them' (E. Grosz, in L. Doan, 1994, 71)

46. Bette Gordon & Karin Kay: "Look Back/ Talk Back", in P. Gibson, 1993, 91.

47. John Kucich, "Moral Authority in the Late Novel: The Gendering of Art", in

H, 224.

48. A. Rich: "Compulsory Heterosexuality and Lesbian Existence", in A. Rich, 1980.

49. Becky Rosa: "Anti-monogamy", 1994, 110.

50. Christobel Mackenzie, 1993, 140.

51. Claudia: "Fear of Pornography", in A. Assiter, 1993, 132.

52. See Colleen Lamos: "The Postmodern Lesbian Position: *On Our Backs*", in L. Doan, 1994, 96; J. Butler, 1990; Case: "Toward a Butch-Femme Aesthetic", in Lynda Hart, ed. *Making a Spectacle: Feminist Essays on Contemporary Women's Theatre*, University of Michigan Press, Ann Arbor 1989.

53. Becky Rosa, 1994, 107.

54. Bette Gordon & Karin Kay: "Look Back/ Talk Back", in P. Gibson, 1993, 95.

55. Kristin Brady: "Textual Hysteria: Hardy's Narrator on Women", in H, 90.

56. Janet Dixon: "Separatism", *Spare Rib*, 192, 1988, 6.

57. See Alice, Gordon, Debbie and Mary: "Separatism", in S. Hoagland, 1988, 31-40; Ti-Grace Atkinson: *Amazon Odyssey*, Links Books, New York 1974; Sally Munt, 1992.

58. M. Wittig: "One is not born a woman", in S. Hoagland, 446-7. Monique Wittig's lesbian materialist analysis of heterosexuality (in *The Straight Mind*) ignores some of the ways in which 'compulsory heterosexuality' can be subverted in a postmodern era. (Cathy Griggers: "Lesbian Bodies in the Age of (Post)-Mechanical Reproduction", in L. Doan, 1994, 124).

59. Daniel R. Schwarz: "Beginnings and Endings in Hardy's Major Fiction", in D. Kramer, 1979, 28.

60. S. Freud: "Drives and their vicissitudes", *Papers on Metapsychology*, 1915.

61. J. Kristeva: "Narcissus: The New Insanity", in *Tales of Love*, 116.

62. J. Kristeva: "Bataille and the Sun, or the Guilty Text", in *Tales of Love*, 368.

63. Perry Meisel: "Interview with Julia Kristeva", tr. Margaret Waller, *Partisan Review*, 51, Winter 1984, 131-2.

64. John Lechte: "Art, Love and Melancholy in the Work of Julia Kristeva", in J. Fletcher, 1990, 24.

3   *Tess of the d'Urbervilles*

1. Jacques Darras writes that 'Tess *is* space, as space is the raw material which is the novelist's concern... Thomas Hardy praises the infinite potentialities of a material feminine imagination in the remarkable microcosmic area of Dorset' (Darras, in L. Butler, 1989, 220).

2. Kathleen Rogers wrote that 'Tess herself is almost less a personality than a beautiful portion of nature violated by human selfishness and over-intellectualizing' (1975, 249).

3. Ovid, *Fasti*, Loeb 1967, iv, 493.

4. M. Higonnet: "A Woman's Story: Tess and the Problem of Voice", in M. Higonnet, 1993, 15.

5. Elisabeth Bronfen: "Pay As You Go: On the Exchange of Bodies and Signs", in H, 81.

6. 'Tess was a scandalous lady in fiction in several respects', writes Christopher Walbank in *Thomas Hardy*, 'As a victim of rape she was the mother of an illegitimate

child and tainted by both in the eyes of the Victorian public' (111).

7. D. Davidson is one of many critics (in "The Traditional Basis of Thomas Hardy's Fiction") to discuss Hardy's use of balladry (in A. Guerard, 1986, 17).

8. The famous phrase about 'the President of the Immortals' at the end of Tess of the d'Urbervilles refers to a hunting metaphor in Classical mythology, from Aeschylus' *Prometheus Bound* (I, 169). For Jean Jacques Lecercle, up until this point, Hardy's narrator in *Tess* has remained relatively distanced, but the 'President of the Immortals' sentence is a moment of 'stylistic violence':

What we have is an explosion of anger, irony giving way to sarcasm and rage, an instance of verbal violence, as if the pent-up energy of a narrator who so far had kept his distance has suddenly been liberated. (in L. Butler, 1989, 1).

9. Angela Carter sees in Tess's mother a representative of the old world of superstition and folklore, which was about to disappear:

he [Hardy] – perfectly consciously – described a way of life at the very moment when profound change was about to begin. Tess and her sisters are themselves whirled away from that rural life deeply rooted in the past into an urban world of ceaseless and giddily accelerating change and innovation, where everything – including, or even especially, our notions of the nature of women and men – was in the melting pot, because the very idea of what constitutes 'human nature' was in the melting pot. (A. Carter, xxi)

10. J.J. Lecercle writes in "The Violence of Style in *Tess of the d'Urbervilles*": 'Tess is the sacrificed witch; she tears the veil of the civilized morality of modern society and provokes a regression to the original, founding violence' (in L. Butler, 1989, 15).

11. L. Irigaray: *Ce sexe qui n'en est pas un*, in E. Marks, 1981, 107.

12. Jane Marcus writes in *Jump Cut* that Tess is 'the great Unwed Mother', the unmarried mother as social outsider. Marcus reckons that when Tess murders Alec women 'weep for joy'. Similarly, when an abused woman hurts or kills her abuser, or is cleared of murdering her abuser in court, women cheer. 'For Tess revenges all the women wronged by men, raped, taken advantage of, impregnated, battered, harrassed and despised for her lost virtue' (1981, 3).

13. Elisabeth Bronfen: "Pay As You Go: On the Exchange of Bodies and Signs", in H, 81.

14. E. Wright, 1989, 119; J. Kristeva, 1982, 237f.

15. For Julia Kristeva, as for Sigmund Freud and Jacques Lacan who tackled the experiences of birth and growth before her, something extraordinary happens in the stages of early growth. Kristeva's outsider artist is sited somewhere between Oedipus and Orpheus, the symbolic and the semiotic. In the 'semiotic' phase, all is flux and incoherence, provisional, inchoate, occasional. Kristeva's *chora* is 'on the borderline between all polarities: between being and nothing, idealism and materialism, sacred and profane, silence and language', writes Philippa Berry (256). It is a pre-linguistic mode, anterior to syntax, denotation, meaning. Then, with the mirror phase and the castration in the Oedipus complex, the individual is enculturated and civilized – language is acquired, and articulation. Importantly, the symbolic is a phase of identification. The symbolic links to the father, to the Law of the Father, the Lacanian *nom/ non du père* ('name/ no of the father'), to symbolic laws, to patriarchal power, to sign, syntax, and social constraints (J. Kristeva, 1982, 6-7). Even though one enters the symbolic, however, the semiotic is never wholly

eliminated. Subjectivity still includes some aspect of the otherness, the alien, marginal and repressed realm. From the *chora* and semiotic, flows poetry. This is where things get very interesting. Artistic creation becomes a struggle involving signification, transgression, the semiotic and the symbolic. The semiotic is revolutionary because of the way in which the psychological subject has been made up since the Enlightenment: the semiotic can be a means of transgressing the (masculine) symbolic (S. Hekman, 1990, 149).

16. There is something inevitably nostalgic about Julia Kristeva's evocation of the semiotic realm, for the semiotic mode 'bears the most archaic memories of our link with the maternal body' ("A Question of Subjectivity", 130).

17. 'In many ways Tess represents the best that human nature has to offer', wrote Benjamin B. Sankey (1965, in A. LaValley, 98).

18. Andrea Dworkin sees women as having one choice – 'lie or die' – not a conspiracy but a forced pretense, because '[w]omen are still basically viewed as sexual chattel – socially, legally, culturally, and in practice' (1988, 229).

19. Franz Stanzel: "Thomas Hardy: *Tess of the d'Urbervilles*", in *Der Moderne Englische Roman*, Berlin, 1963, 38f.

20. L. Irigaray: *Ce sexe qui n'en est pas un*, in E. Marks, 1981, 105.

21. Elisabeth Bronfen: "Pay As You Go: On the Exchange of Bodies and Signs", in H, 67.

22. See S. Gatrell, 133; T. Hardy: "Candour in English Fiction", Per, 16-19. Hardy was censored (though he knew he would be in serial magazine publications); he felt he couldn't say things the way he would have liked to. Sue never says 'fuck life', though it seems she wants to say it, at times, like the old woman in Samuel Beckett's *Rockaby* who says 'fuck life' at the end of the play.

23. M. Duras, interview, *Signs*, Winter 1975, in E. Marks, 175.

24. Similar crude symbolism occurs when Tess compassionately kills the maimed pheasants (352). Pheasants, those soft, plump and beautiful birds, the targets of men of leisure (in Britain they are still reared and hunted mainly by middle-aged white men), will later bring Connie and Mellors together in D.H. Lawrence's last novel.

25. Alec says:
- '"it is better that I could not look too often on you"' (388);
- '"swear you will never tempt me"' (390);
- '"Tess – don't look at me so – I can't stand your looks"' (396);
- '"It is hard that a good woman should do harm to a bad man"' (399);
- '"why then have you tempted me? ...surely there was never such a maddening mouth since Eve's"' (402);
- '"*I* trouble *you*? I think I may ask, why do you trouble me?"' (408);
- '"you work upon me, perhaps to my complete perdition"' (409);
- '"You have been the cause of my backsliding"' (411).

26. D.H. Lawrence: *A Study of Thomas Hardy*, in 1971, 222f.

27. In the American *Harper's Weekly* serial version, Thomas Hardy left out the fake registrar sequence which had appeared in the British *Graphic* serialization, and had Tess explaining that her marriage to Alec was by 'special licence', after being 'pestered' and 'persecuted' by Alec (S. Gatrell, 1988, 95).

28. Irving Howe wrote: '[n]othing matters in the novel nearly so much as Tess herself' (1985). Bernard J. Paris wrote that Thomas Hardy 'presents almost everything from her point of view... Hardy is Tess's apologist: he sees her and everything

else in her terms' (quoted in J. Laird, 1975, 122).

29. Rosemarie Morgan wrote in *Women and Sexuality in the Novels of Thomas Hardy* that 'from Havelock Ellis to Roman Polanski it is the dumb, gentle, unthinking, passive Tess who too often survives in interpretation.' And she adds: '[t]his defeats Hardy's purposes entirely. There is no denunciation, in his entire œuvre, as unequivocal as his denunciation of the sexual double-standard in *Tess*' (1988, 84). According to Morgan, Hardy sees Tess as 'complex, diverse, unique: fierce and gentle, regenerative and destructive, trusting and suspicious, philosophical, mystical and sexy' (ib., 98).

30. For John Goode, in "Women and the literary text", the reader observes and is implicated in 'the objectification of Tess by the narrator which is acted out in the novel' (1976, 253).

BIBLIOGRAPHY

All books are published in London, England, unless otherwise stated.

THOMAS HARDY

Tess of the D'Urbervilles, ed. David Skilton, Penguin, 1978/85
Tess of the D'Urbervilles: An Authoritative Text, Hardy and the Novel, ed. Scott Elledge, W.W. Norton & Co, New York, NY, 1965/79
Tess of the d'Urbervilles, eds. Juliet Grindle & Simon Gatrell, Oxford University Press, 1983
Tess of the d'Urbervilles, World Classics, eds. Juliet Grindle & Simon Gatrell, Oxford University Press, 1988
"*Tess of the d'Urbervilles*", *Graphic*, XLIV, July-December, 1891
Jude the Obscure, ed. Patricia Ingham, Oxford University Press, 1985
Jude the Obscure: An Authoritative Text, Backgrounds and Sources, Criticism, ed. Norman Page, W.W. Norton & Co, New York, NY, 1978
The Return of the Native, ed. George Woodcock, Penguin, 1978
The Woodlanders, ed. James Gibson, Penguin, 1981
The Mayor of Casterbridge, ed. Martin Seymour-Smith, Penguin, 1985
Under the Greenwood Tree, ed. Simon Gatrell, Oxford University Press, 1985
A Pair of Blue Eyes, ed. Alan Manford, Oxford University Press, 1985
The Well-Beloved, ed. Tom Hetherington, Oxford University Press, 1986
Two on a Tower, ed. F.B. Pinion, Macmillan, London, 1975
A Laocidean, Heron/ Macmillan, London, 1987
The Hand of Ethelberta, ed. Robert Gittings, Macmillan, London, 1975
The Trumpet-Major, St Martins Library, Macmillan, London, 1962
Complete Poems, ed. James Gibson, Macmillan, London, 1981
Selected Poems, ed. Walford Davies, Dent, 1982
Selected Short Poems, ed. John Wain, Macmillan, London, 1966/75
The Gates Along the Path: Poems, Terra Nova Editions, 1979
Hardy's Love Poems, ed. Carl J. Weber, Macmillan, London, 1983

The Short Stories of Thomas Hardy, Macmillan, London, 1928
The Literary Notebooks of Thomas Hardy, ed. Lennart A. Björk, 2 vols, Macmillan, 1985
The Collected Letters of Thomas Hardy, eds. Richard Little Purdy & Michael Millgate, 7 vols, Clarendon Press, 1978-88
Thomas Hardy's Notebooks, ed. Evelyn Hardy, Hogarth Press, 1955
The Personal Notebooks of Thomas Hardy, ed. Richard H. Taylor, Macmillan, London, 1978
The Life of Thomas Hardy, Macmillan, London, 1962
The Life and Work of Thomas Hardy, ed. Michael Millgate, Macmillan, London, 1984
Personal Writings, ed. Harold Orel, Macmillan, London, 1967
Thomas Hardy's "Studies, Specimens &c" Notebook, eds. P. Dalziel & M. Millgate, Clarendon Press, Oxford, 1994
Thomas Hardy's Public Voice, ed. M. Millgate, Clarendon Press, Oxford, 2001

OTHERS

D. Abraham. "Clarissa and Tess: Two Meanings of Death", *Massachusetts Studies in English*, 1, 1968
J. Adamson. "Tess, Time and Its Shapings", *The Critical Review*, 26, 1984
Gary Adelman. *Jude the Obscure: A Paradise of Despair*, Twayne, New York, NY, 1992
John Alcorn. *The Nature Novel from Hardy to Lawrence*, Macmillan, London, 1973
Patricia Alden. *Social Mobility in the English Bildungsroman*, UMI Research Press, Ann Arbor, 1986
A. Alexander. *Thomas Hardy: The "Dream-Country"of His Fiction*, London: Vision, 1987.
B.J. Alexander. "Anti-Christian Elements in Thomas Hardy's Novels", *DAI*, 36, 1975
P. Allingham. "The Original Illustrations for Hardy's *Tess of the d'Urbervilles*: Drawn by Daniel A. Wehrschmidt, Ernest Borough-Johnson, and Joseph Syddall for the *Graphic*, 1891", *Thomas Hardy Yearbook*, 24, 1998
—. "Six Original Illustrations for Hardy's *Tess of the d'Urbervilles* Drawn by Sir Hubert Von Herkomer, R. A., for the *Graphic*, 1891", *The Thomas Hardy Journal* 10,1, 1994
Wayne Anderson. "The Rhetoric of Silence in Hardy's Fiction", *Studies in the Novel*, 17, 1985
J. Anonby. "Hardy's Handling of Biblical Allusions in His Portrayal of Tess in *Tess of the d'Urbervilles*", *Christianity and Literature*, 30, 3, 1981
T. Armstrong. *Haunted Hardy*, Palgrave Macmillan, London, 2000
Alison Assister & Avedon Carol, eds. *Bad Girls and Dirty Pictures: The Challenge to Reclaim Feminism*, Pluto Press, 1993
D.F. Barber, ed. *Concerning Thomas Hardy*, Charles Skilton, 1968
J.O. Bailey. *The Poetry of Thomas Hardy*, University of North Carolina Press, Chapel Hill 1970
A. Banerjee, ed. *An Historical Evaluation of Thomas Hardy's Poetry*, Edwin Mellen Press, 2001
N. Barber & P. Lee-Browne. *Thomas Hardy*, Evans Brothers, 2000
Regina Barreca, ed. *Sex and Death in Victorian Literature*, Indiana University Press,

Bloomington, 1990

John Barrell. "Geographies of Hardy's Wessex", *Journal of Historical Geography*, 8, 1982

John Bayley. *An Essay on Hardy*, Cambridge University Press, 1978

C. Beckingham. "The Importance of the Family in Hardy's Fictional World", *The Thomas Hardy Journal*, 5,2, 1989

S. Beliveau. "Rethinking English Naturalism: Feminine Decadence, Hardy's *Tess* and the French Context", *Excavatio: Emile Zola and Naturalism*, 11, 1998

R. Bell & R. Klein, eds. *Radically Speaking: Feminism Reclaimed*, Spinifex, North Melbourne, 1996

T. Bender. "Competing Cultural Domains, Borderlands and Spatial/ Temporal Thresholds in Hardy, Conrad, and D. H. Lawrence", *REAL: The Yearbook of Research in English and American Literature*, 21, 2005

R. Benzing. "In Defence of Tess", *Contemporary Review*, 218, 1971

S. Berger. *Thomas Hardy and Visual Structures: Framing, Disruption, Process*, New York University Press, New York, NY, 1990.

S. Bernstein. "Confessing and Editing: The Politics of Purity in Hardy's Tess", in *Virginal Sexuality and Textuality in Victorian Literature*, ed. Lloyd Davis, State University of New York Press, Albany, 1993

Philippa Berry & Andrew Wernick, eds. *Shadow of Spirit: Postmodernism and Religion*, Routledge, 1992

Kathleen Blake. "Pure Tess: Thomas Hardy on Knowing a Woman", *Studies in English Literature*, 22, 1982

Paula Blank. "*Tess of the d'Urbervilles*": The English Novel and the Foreign Plot", *Mid-Hudson Language Studies*, 12, 1989

Harold Bloom, ed. *Thomas Hardy: Modern Critical Views*, Chelsea House, New York, NY, 1987

—. ed. *Thomas Hardy's Tess of the d'Urbervilles*, Chelsea House Publishers, New York, NY, 1996

—. *Thomas Hardy*, Chelsea House Publishers, New York, NY, 2003

E. Blunden. *Thomas Hardy*, London, 1942

R. Blythe. *Characters and Their Landscapes*, Harcout Brace Jovanovitch, New York, NY, 1983

T. Boll. "Tess as an Animal in Nature", *English Literature in Transition, 1880-1920*, 9, 1966

Charlotte Bonica. "Nature and Paganism in Hardy's Tess", *Journal of English Literary History*, 49, 4 1982

W. Bonnell. "Broken Communion in *Tess of the d'Urbervilles*", *English Language Notes*, 31, 4, 1994

F. Bonner et al, eds. *Imagining Women Cultural Representations and Gender*, Polity Press, Cambridge, 1992

Penny Boumelha. *Thomas Hardy and Women: Sexual Ideology and Narrative*, Harvester, 1982

A. Brick. "Paradise and Consciousness in Hardy's Tess", *19th Century Fiction*, 17, 1962

J. Bristow & A. Wilson, eds. *Activating Theory, Gay, Bisexual Politics*, Lawrence & Wishart, London, 1993

—. *Effeminate England: Homosexuality After 1885*, Open University Press, Milton Keynes, 1995

Jean Brooks. *Thomas Hardy: The Poetic Structure*, Elek, 1971

B. Brown & P. Adams: "The feminine body and feminist politics", *M/F*, 3, 1979
Douglas Brown. *Thomas Hardy,* Longmans, Green & Co., 1954
—. *Thomas Hardy: 'The Mayor of Casterbridge'*, Arnold, 1962
S.H. Brown. ""Tess" and Tess: An Experiment in Genre", *Modern Fiction Studies,* 28, 1, 1982
J.H. Buckley. "Tess and the d'Urbervilles", *Victorian Institute Journal,* 20, 1992
J.B. Bullen. *The Expressive Eye: Fiction of Perception in the Work of Thomas Hardy,* Clarendon Press, 1986
Peter J. Burgard, ed. *Nietzsche and the Feminine,* University Press, of Virginia, Charlottesville, 1994
L. Bushloper. "Hardy's *Tess of the D'Urbervilles,*" *Explicator,* 52:4, 1994
Judith Butler. *Gender Trouble: Feminism and the Subversion of Identity,* Routledge, 1990
Lance St. John Butler, ed. *Thomas Hardy, After Fifty Years,* Macmillan, London, 1977
—. *Thomas Hardy,* Cambridge University Press, 1978
—. ed. *Alternative Hardy,* Macmillan, London, 1989
B. Caminero-Santangelo. "A Moral Dilemma: Ethics in *Tess of the d'Urbervilles*", *English Studies: A Journal of English Language and Literature,* 75, 1, 1994
Elizabeth Campbell. "*Tess of the d'Urbervilles*: Misfortune Is a Woman", *Victorian Newsletter,* 70, 1989
A. Carroll. "Human Milk in the Modern World: Breastfeeding and the Cult of the Dairy in *Adam Bede* and *Tess of the d'Urbervilles*", *Women's Studies: An Interdisciplinary Journal* 31,2, 2002
Glen Cavaliero. *The Rural Tradition in the English Novel 1900-1939,* Macmillan, London, 1977
Joseph Campbell. *The Masks of God: Creative Mythology,* Penguin, London, 1976
—. *The Power of Myth,* with Bill Moyers, ed. B.S. Flowers, Doubleday, New York, NY, 1988
—. *This business of the gods...,* Windrose Films, Ontario, 1989
Richard Carpenter. *Thomas Hardy,* Macmillan, London, 1978
Norman T. Carrington. *The Mayor of Casterbridge,* Pan, 1976
Peter J. Casagrande. *Hardy's Influence on the Modern Novel,* Palgrave Macmillan, London, 1987
—. *Unity in Thomas Hardy's Novels,* Regents, Lawrence, 1982
—. *Tess of the d'Urbervilles: Unorthodox Beauty,* Twayne, New York, NY, 1992
David Cecil. *Hardy the Novelist,* Constable, 1943
J. Chandler, ed. *Thomas Hardy's Christmas,* Sutton Publishing, 1997
S. Chandra. *Thomas Hardy,* Sangam Books, 1999
R. Chapman. *The Language of Thomas Hardy,* Macmillan, London, 1990
Mary E. Chase. *Thomas Hardy From Serial to Novel,* University of Minnesota Press, 1927
Gail Chester & Julienne Dickey, ed. *Feminism and Censorship: The Current Debate,* Prism Press, Bridport, Dorset, 1988
Mary Childers. "Thomas Hardy, the Man Who 'Liked' Women", *Criticism,* 23, 1981
Hélène Cixous. *The Hélène Cixous Reader,* ed. Susan Sellers, Blackwell, 1994
—. *The Newly Born Woman,* tr. Betsy Wing, Minnesota University Press, Minneapolis, 1986
J. Clarke. "More Light on the Serial Publication of *Tess of the d'Urbervilles*", *Review of English Studies,* 54, 213, 2003
Laura Claridge. "Tess: A Less Than Pure Woman Ambivalently Presented", *Texas*

Studies in Literature and Language, 28, 3, 1986
—. & Elizabeth Langland, eds. *Out of Bounds: Male Writers and Gender(ed) Criticism,* University Massachusetts Press, Amherst, 1990
G. Clarke, ed. *Thomas Hardy: Critical Assessments,* Helm Information, 1993
P. Clements & J. Grindle, eds. *The Poetry of Thomas Hardy,* London, 1980
D. Collins. *Thomas Hardy and His God: A Liturgy of Unbelief,* Macmillan, London, 1990
Vere H. Collins. *Talks With Thomas Hardy at Max Gate,* Duckworth, 1972
Alex Comfort. *I and That,* Beazley, 1979
B. Cortus *et al.* "Hardy: Drama and Movies: Arts and Entertainment's *Tess,* Dialogues from 1998", *Hardy Review,* 4, 2001
W.V. Costanzo. "Polanski in Wessex: Filming *Tess of the d'Urbervilles*", *Literature/Film Quarterly,* 9, 2, 1981
J. Stevens Cox, ed. *Thomas Hardy Yearbook,* Toucan Press, various dates
R.G. Cox, ed. *Thomas Hardy: The Critical Heritage,* Barnes & Noble 1970
—. ed. *Thomas Hardy: The Critical Heritage,* Routledge, 1996
R. Craik. "Hardy's *Tess of the D'Urbervilles*", *Explicator,* 53:1, 1994
Louis Crompton. "The Sunburnt God: Ritual and Tragic Myth in *The Return of the Native*", *Boston University Studies in English,* 4, 1960
Gail Cunningham. *The New Woman and the Victorian Novel,* Macmillan, London, 1978
V. Cunningham. "Tess, *Tess of the d'Urbervilles,* Thomas Hardy, 1891", *The Novel: Volume 2: Forms and Themes,* ed. Franco Moretti, Princeton University Press, Princeton, NJ, 2006
H.M. Daleski. "*Tess*: Mastery and Abandon", *Essays in Criticism,* 30, 1980
—. *Thomas Hardy and Paradoxes of Love,* University of Missouri Press, Columbia, MO, 1997
C. Daniel. "Science, Misogyny, and *Tess of the d'Urbervilles*", *Hardy Review,* 1, 1998
—. "Orpheus, Eurydice and *Tess of the d'Urbervilles*", *Thomas Hardy Journal,* 16,1, 2000
Jagdish Chandra Dave. *The Human Predicament in Hardy's Novels,* Macmillan, London, 1985
Donald Davie. *Thomas Hardy and British Poetry,* Routledge & Kegan Paul, 1979
—. *With the Grain: Essays on Thomas Hardy and Modern British Poetry,* Carcanet Press, Manchester, 1998
W. Davis, Jr. "'But He Can Be Prosecuted for This': Legal and Sociological Backgrounds of the Mock Marriage in Hardy's Serial *Tess*", *Colby Library Quarterly,* 25,1, 1989
—. "Hardy and the 'Deserted Wife' Question: The Failure of the Law in *Tess of the d'Urbervilles*", *Colby Quarterly,* 29,1, 1993
—. "The Rape of Tess: Hardy, English Law, and the Case for Sexual Assault", *Nineteenth Century Literature,* 52:2, 1997
W. Davis. "'Strange and Godlike Power': Music in *Tess of the d'Urbervilles*", *Hardy Review,* 2, 1999
Lois Deacon & Terry Coleman. *Providence and Mr. Hardy,* Hutchinson, 1966
D. De Laura. "The Ache of Modernism in Hardy's Later Novels", Sept, 1967
B. DeMille. "Cruel Illusions: Nietzsche, Conrad, Hardy, and the 'Shadowy Ideal'", *SEL,* 30:4, 1990
Joanna Devereux. *Patriarchy and Its Discontents: Sexual Politics in Selected Novels and Stories of Thomas Hardy,* Routledge, 2003

Laura Doan, ed. *The Lesbian Postmodern*, Columbia University Press, New York, NY, 1994

Mary Ann Doane. *The Desire to Desire: The Woman's Film of the 1940's*, Macmillan, London, 1987

Tim Dolin & Peter Widdowson, eds. *Thomas Hardy and Contemporary Literary Studies*, Palgrave Macmillan, 2004

Margaret Drabble, ed. *The Genius of Thomas Hardy*, Weidenfeld & Nicolson, 1976

J. Drake. *Thomas Hardy*, Wessex Books, 1999

—. ed. *A Writer's Britain*, Thames & Hudson, 1979

R.P. Draper, ed. *Thomas Hardy: Three Pastoral Novels*, Macmillan, London, 1987

—. ed. *Hardy: The Tragic Novels*, Macmillan, London, 1975

H.C. Duffin. *Thomas Hardy*, Greenwood Press, Conn., 1978

S. Dutta. *Ambivalence in Hardy*, Palgrave Macmillan, London, 1999

A. Dworkin. *Right-Wing Women: The Politics of Domesticated Females*, Women's Press 1983

—. *Pornography: Men Possessing Women*, Women's Press 1984

—. *Ice and Fire*, Flamingo 1987

—. *Women's Equality*, Organizing Against Pornography, Minneapolis 1988

—. *Letters From a War Zone*, Secker & Warburg 1988

—. *Intercourse*, Arrow 1988

—. and Catherine MacKinnon: *Pornography and Civil Rights: A New Day for Women's Equality*, 1988

Mary Eagleton, ed. *Feminist Literary Criticism*, Longman, 1991

Terry Eagleton. "Thomas Hardy: Nature as Language", *Critical Quarterly*, Summer, 1971

—. *The Eagleton Reader*, Blackwell, Oxford, 1998

Roger Ebbatson. *Lawrence and the Nature Tradition*, Harvester Press, Brighton 1980

—. "The Plutonic Master: Hardy and the Steam Threshing Machine", *Critical Survey*, 2, 1990

—. *Hardy: The Margin of the Unexpressed*, Sheffield Academic Press, 1994

S. Eddy. *Thomas Hardy (Pre-1914 Classics Series)*, Folens Publishers, 2000

Anne-Marie Edwards. *Discovering Hardy's Wessex*, BBC, 1978

—. & Michael Edwards. *In the Steps of Thomas Hardy*, Jones Books, 2003

D. Eggenschwiler. "Eustacia Vye, Queen of the Night and Courtly Pretender", *Nineteenth Century Fiction*, 25, 1971

H. Eilberg-Schwartz & W. Doniger, eds. *Off With Her Head! The Denial of Women's Identity in Myth, Religion, and Culture*, University of California Press, Berkeley, 1995

M. Elbert. "Malinowski's Reading List: Tess as Field Guide to Woman", *Colby Quarterly*, 35,1, 1999

Ralph W.V. Elliott. *Thomas Hardy's English*, Basil Blackwell, 1984

D. Ellis & H. Mills. *D.H. Lawrence's Non-Fiction: Art, Thought and Genre*, Cambridge University Press, Cambridge, 1988

—. *D.H. Lawrence: The Dying Game, 1922-30*, Cambridge University Press, Cambridge, 1998

A. Enstice. *Thomas Hardy*, London, 1979

R. Evans. "The Other Eustacia", *Novel*, 1, 1968

M. Faber. "Tess and the Rape of Lucrece", *English Language Notes*, 5, 1968

M. Farwell. *Heterosexual Plots and Lesbian Narratives*, New York University Press, 1996

C. Fierz. "Polanski Misses: A Critical Essay Concerning Polansky's Reading of Hardy's *Tess*", *Literature/Film Quarterly* 27, 2, 1999

A. Fischler. "An Affinity for Birds: Kindness in Hardy's *Jude the Obscure*", *Studies in the Novel,* 13:3, 1981

—. "Gins and Spirits: The Letter's Edge in Hardy's *Jude the Obscure*", *Studies in the Novel,* 16:1, 1984

Joe Fisher. *The Hidden Hardy,* Macmillan, London, 1992

Alexander Fischler. "Gins and Spirits: The Letter's Edge in Hardy's *Jude the Obscure*", *SNNTS*, 16, 1984

John Fletcher & Andrew Benjamin, ed. *Abjection, Melancholia and Love: the Work of Julia Kristeva*, Routledge, 1990

John Fowles & Jo Draper. *Thomas Hardy's England,* Cape, 1984

D. Franke. "Hardy's Ur-Priestess and the Phases of a Novel", *Studies in the Novel,* 39, 2, 2007

Janet Freeman. "Ways of Looking at Tess", *Studies in Philology,* 79, 3, 1982

Alan Friedman. *The Turn of the Novel,* Oxford University Press, 1966

—. ed. *Forms of Modern Fiction,* Austin, 1975

D. Galef. *Tess of the d'Urbervilles/ Thomas Hardy,* New York, NY: Barnes & Noble, 2005

Lorraine Gamman & Margaret Marshment, eds. *The Female Gaze: Women as Viewers of Popular Culture,* Women's Press 1988

M. Garber. *Vested Interests: Cross-Dressing and Cultural Anxiety,* Routledge, London, 1992

—. *Vice Versa: Bisexuality and the Eroticism of Everyday Life,* Simon & Schuster, NY, 1995

Marjorie Garson. *Hardy's Fables of Integrity: Woman, Body, Text,* Oxford University Press, 1991

Simon Gatrell, ed. *The Thomas Hardy Archive 1: Tess of the d'Urbervilles,* Garland, New York, NY, 1986

—. *Hardy the Creator: A Textual Biography,* Clarendon Press, 1988

—. *Thomas Hardy and the Proper Study of Mankind,* Macmillan, London, 1993

—. "Dress, Body and Psyche in 'the Romantic Adventures of a Milkmaid': *Tess of the d'Urbervilles* and the *Mayor of Casterbridge*", *Thomas Hardy Journal,* 22 , 2006

E. Gemmette. "George Eliot's *Mill on the Floss* and Hardy's *Jude the Obscure*", *Explicator,* 42:3, 1984

Helmut E. Gerber & W. Eugene Davis, eds. *Thomas Hardy: An Annotated Bibliography of Writings About Him,* Northern Illinois University Press, 1973

James Gibson, ed. *Thomas Hardy and History,* Palgrave Macmillan, London, 1974

—. & Trevor Johnson, eds. *Thomas Hardy: Poems: A Casebook,* Macmillan, 1979

—. *Thomas Hardy,* Palgrave Macmillan, London, 1996

Pamela Church Gibson & Roma Gibson, eds. *Dirty Looks: Women, Pornography, Power,* British Film Institute, 1993

R. Giddings & E. Sheen, eds. *The Classic Novel From Page to Screen,* Manchester University Press, 2000

Robert Gittings. *Young Thomas Hardy,* London, 1975

—. *The Older Hardy,* Heinemann, 1978

—. & J. Manton: *The Second Mrs Hardy,* London, 1979

John Goode. "Sue Bridehead and the New Woman", in M. Jacobus, 1979

—. *Thomas Hardy: The Offensive Truth,* Basil Blackwell, 1988

W. Goetz. "Felicity and Infelicity of Marriage in *Tess of the d'Urbervilles*", *Nineteenth*

Century Fiction, 38, 1983
William Greenslade. *Degeneration, Culture and the Novel 1880-1940*, Cambridge, 1994
Ian Gregor. *The Great Web*, Faber, 1974
J. Gribble. "The Quiet Women of Egdon Heath", *Essays In Criticism*, 46, 1996
Gabriele Griffin et al, eds. *Stirring It: Challenges For Feminism*, Taylor & Francis, 1994
E. Grosz. "Philosophy, Subjectivity and the Body", in C. Pateman & E. Grosz, eds., *Feminist Challenges*, Allen & Unwin, Sydney, 1986
—. "Desire, the body and recent French feminism", *Intervention*, 21-2, 1988
—. *Sexual Subversions*, Allen & Unwin, London, 1989
—. "The Body of Signification", in J. Fletcher, 1990
—. *Jacques Lacan: A Feminist Introduction*, Routledge, London, 1990
—. "Lesbian fetishism?", *Differences*, 3, 2, 1991
—. "Fetishization", in E. Wright, 1992
—. "Julia Kristeva", in E. Wright, 1992
—. *Voltaile Bodies,* Indiana University Press, Bloomington, 1994
—. "Refiguring Lesbian Desire", in L. Doan, 1994
—. *Space, Time and Perversion*, Routledge, London, 1995
Peter Grundy. "Linguistics and Literary Criticism: A Marriage of Convenience", *English*, 30, 137, 1981
Albert J. Guerard. *Thomas Hardy*, Oxford University Press, 1949
—. ed. *Hardy: A Collection of Critical Essays,* Prentice-Hall International, New York, NY, 1963/86
A. Gussow,. "Dreaming Holmberry-Lipped Tess: Aboriginal Reverie and Spectatorial Desire in *Tess of the d'Ubervilles*", *Studies in the Novel*, 32, 4, 2000
F.E. Halliday. *Thomas Hardy,* Adams & Dart, Bath, 1972
—. *Thomas Hardy: His Life and Work,* House of Stratus, 2001
G. Handley. *Thomas Hardy: Tess of the d'Urbervilles,* Penguin Critical Studies, Penguin, 1991
R. Hand. "'Self-Adaptation' and the Literature of Region and Nation: Hardy's *Tess of the d'Urbervilles*", *Swansea Review*, 1994
T. Hands, T. *Thomas Hardy: Distracted Preacher?,* London, 1989
—. *A Hardy Chronology* London, 1992
—. *Thomas Hardy*, Macmillan, London, 1995
C. Harbinson. "Echoes of Keats' *Lamia* in Hardy's *Tess of the d'Urbervilles*", *Notes and Queries*, 49 247,1, 2002
B. Hardy. *Thomas Hardy*, Athlone, London, 2000
Evelyn Hardy. *The Countryman's Ear,* Tebb House, Padstow, Cornwall, 1982
Margaret Harris. "Thomas Hardy's *Tess of the d'Urbervilles*: Faithfully presented by Roman Polanski", *Sydney Studies in English*, 7, 1982
L. Hart. *Between the Body and the Flesh: Performing Sadomasochism*, Columbia University Press, 1998
G. Harvey. *The Complete Critical Guide to Thomas Hardy*, Routledge, London, 2003
M.E. Hassett. "Compromised Romanticism in *Jude the Obscure*", *Nineteenth Century Fiction*, 25, 1971
Desmond Hawkins. *Hardy's Wessex*, Macmillan, London, 1983
—. *Hardy: Novelist and Poet,* David & Charles, Devon, 1976
Jeremy Hawthorn, ed. *The Nineteenth-Century British Novel*, Arnold 1986
Stephen Hazell, ed. *The English Novel*, Macmillan, London, 1978
J. Hazen. "The Tragedy of Tess Durbeyfield", *Texas Studies in Literature and Language,*

11, 1969

J. Heffernan. "'Cruel Persuasion': Seduction, Temptation and Agency in Hardy's *Tess*", *Thomas Hardy Yearbook*, 35, 2005

R. Heilman. "Hardy's Sue Bridehead", *Nineteenth Century Fiction*, 20, 1966

Susan J. Hekman. *Gender and Knowledge: Elements of a Postmodern Feminism*, Polity Press, 1990

M. Hennelly. "The 'Original Tess': Pre-Texts, Tess, Fess, Tesserae, Carnivalesque", *Thomas Hardy Yearbook*, 25, 1998

Lucille Herbert. "Hardy's Views in Tess of the d'Urbervilles", *English Literary History*, 37, 1970

Margaret R. Higonnet, ed."Fictions of Feminine Voice: Antiphony and Silence in Hardy's *Tess of the d'Urbervilles*", in L. Claridge, 1990

—. *The Sense of Sex: Feminist Perspectives on Hardy*, University of Illinois Press, Urbana, 1993

G.G. Hiller, ed. *Poems of the Elizabethan Age*, Methuen, 1977

Sarah Lucia Hoagland & Julia Penelope, eds. *For Lesbians Only: A separatist anthology*, Onlywomen Press, 1988

Bert G. Hornback. *The Metaphor of Chance: Vision and Technique in the Works of Thomas Hardy*, Ohio University Press, Athens, 1971

L. Horne. "Symbol and Structure in *Jude the Obscure*", *Literatur in Wissenschaft und Unterricht*, 11, 1978

Irving Howe. *Thomas Hardy*, Macmillan, London, 1985

Maggie Humm. *Feminisms: A Reader*, Harvester Wheatsheaf, 1992

—. *Practising Feminist Criticism*, Prentice-Hall 1995

—. ed. *A Reader's Guide to Contemporary Feminist Literary Criticism*, Prentice-Hall 1995

—. ed. *The Dictionary of Feminist Theory*, Harvester Wheatsheaf, 1989/ 1995

J. Humma. "Language and Disguise: The Imagery of Nature and Sex in *Tess*", *South Atlantic Review*, 54, 4, 1989

Virginia R. Hyman. *Ethical Perspectives in the Novels of Thomas Hardy*, Kenniket Press, New York, NY, 1975

S. Hynes. *The Pattern of Hardy's Poetry*, London, 1961

D. Ifkovic. "Tess as an Innocent", *Thomas Hardy Journal*, 18, 3, 2002

Patricia Ingham. *Thomas Hardy*, Harvester Wheatsheaf, Hemel Hempstead 1989

—. *Thomas Hardy*, Oxford University Press, 2003

Luce Irigaray. *This Sex Which Is Not One*, tr. C. Porter & C. Burke, Cornell University Press, New York, NY, 1977

—. *Speculum of the Other Woman*, tr. G.C. Gill, Cornell University Press, New York, NY, 1985

—. *The Irigaray Reader*, ed. Margaret Whitford, Blackwell, Oxford, 1991

—. *Je, tu, nous: Toward a Culture of Difference*, tr. Alison Martin, Routledge, 1993

—. *Thinking the Difference: For a Peaceful Revolution*, Athlone Press, 1994

M. Irwin. *Reading Hardy's Landscapes*, Palgrave Macmillan, London, 2000

Arlene M. Jackson. *Illustration and the Novels of Thomas Hardy*, Macmillan, London, 1981

S. Jackson & J. Jones, eds. *Contemporary Feminist Theories*, Edinburgh University Press, 1998

Mary Jacobus. "Sue the Obscure", *Essays in Criticism*, 25, 1975

—. "Tess's Purity", *Essays in Criticism*, 26, 1976

—. ed. *Women Writing and Writing About Women*, Croom Helm, 1979

—. "Tess: The Making of a Pure Woman", in Bloom, 1987
—. "Hardy's Magian Retrospective", *Essays in Criticism,* 32, 1982
—. *Reading Woman: essays in feminist criticism,* Methuen, 1986
G.M. Jantzen. *Becoming Divine: Towards a Feminist Philosophy of Religion,* Manchester University Press, 1998
J. Jedrzejewski. *Thomas Hardy and the Church,* Palgrave Macmillan, London, 1995
Trevor Johnson. *Thomas Hardy,* Evans Brothers, 1968
Ann Rosalind Jones. "Writing the Body: Toward an Understanding of L'Écriture féminine", in E. Showalter, 1986
J. Juffer. *At Home With Pornography: Women, Sex and Everyday Life,* New York University Press, 1998
C.G. Jung: *Memories, Dreams, Reflections,* Collins, 1967
S. Kang. "[the Laugh of 'Liza-Lu: The Potential Textual Dynamics of *Tess of the d'Urbervilles*]", *Nineteenth Century Literature in English,* 2, 1999
Denis Kay-Robinson. *The Landscape of Thomas Hardy,* Webb & Bower, 1987
—. *Hardy's Wessex Reappraised,* David & Charles, Newton Abbot, Devon 1972
—. *The First Mrs Thomas Hardy,* London, 1979
W.J. Keith. *Regions of the Imagination: The Development of the British Rural Tradition,* University of Toronto Press, Toronto, 1988
—. *The Poetry of Nature: Rural Perspectives in Poetry From Wordsworth to the Present,* University of Toronto Press, Toronto, 1980
A. Kettle. *Hardy the Novelist,* University of Wales Press, Swansea, 1967
James Kincaid: "Hardy's Absences", in D. Kramer, 1979
M. Kinkead-Weekes, ed. *Twentieth-Century Interpretations of The Rainbow,* Prentice-Hall, New Jersey, 1971
—. *D.H. Lawrence: Triumph to Exile, 1912-1922,* Cambridge University Press, Cambridge, 1996
S. Kozloff. "Where Wessex Meets New England: Griffith's *Way Down East* and Hardy's *Tess of the d'Urbervilles*", *Literature/Film Quarterly,* 13, 1, 1985
Dale Kramer. *Thomas Hardy: The Forms of Tragedy,* Macmillan, London, 1975
—. ed. *Critical Approaches to the Fiction of Thomas Hardy,* Barnes, Totowa, 1979
—. ed. *Critical Essays on Thomas Hardy: The Novels,* G.K Hall, 1990
—. *Tess of the d'Urbervilles,* Cambridge University Press, 1991
—. ed. *The Cambridge Companion to Thomas Hardy,* Cambridge University Press, Cambridge, 1999
Julia Kristeva. *About Chinese Women,* tr. A. Barrows, Boyars, 1977
—. *Desire in Language: A Semiotic Approach to Literature and Art,* ed. Leon Roudiez, tr. Thomas Gora, Alice Jardine & Leon Roudiez, Blackwell, 1982
—. *Powers of Horror: An Essay on Abjection,* tr. Leon S. Roudiez, Columbia University Press, New York, NY, 1982
—. *Revolution in Poetic Language,* tr. Margaret Walker, Columbia University Press, New York, NY, 1984
—. *The Kristeva Reader,* ed. Toril Moi, Blackwell, 1986
—. *Tales of Love,* tr. Leon S. Roudiez, Columbia University Press, New York, NY, 1987
—. *In the Beginning Was Love: Psychoanalysis and Faith,* tr. Arthur Goldhammer, Columbia University Press, New York, NY, 1988
—. *Black Sun: Depression and Melancholy,* tr. L.S. Roudiez, Columbia University Press, New York, NY, 1989
—. *Strangers to Ourselves,* tr. L.S. Roudiez, Harvester Wheatsheaf, Hemel

Hempstead, 1991
—. "A Question of Subjectivity: an interview" [with Susan Sellers], *Women's Review*, 12, 1986, in P. Rice, 1992
—. *The Portable Kristeva*, ed. K. Oliver, Columbia University Press, New York, 1997/2002
John Kucich: "Moral Authority in the Late Novel: The Gendering of Art", in M. Higonnet, 1993
Annette Kuhn. "Introduction to Hélène Cixous's Castration or Decapitation?", *Signs*, 7, 1, 1981
—. *Women's Pictures: Feminism and the Cinema*, Routledge & Kegan Paul, 1982
M. Kurata. "Hardy's *Tess of the d'Ubervilles*", *Explicator*, 42,1, 1983
Weston La Barre. *The Ghost Dance*, Allen & Unwin, 1972
—. *Muelos*, Columbia University Press, New York, NY, 1985
Jacques Lacan and the *École Freudienne: Feminine Sexuality*, ed. Juliet Mitchell and Jacqueline Rose, Macmillan, London, 1982
—. *Écrits: A Selection*, tr. Alan Sheridan, Tavistock, 1977
J.T. Laird. *The Shaping of "Tess of the d'Urbervilles"*, Oxford University Press, 1975
—. "New Light on the Evolution of *Tess of the d'Urbervilles*", *Review of English Studies*, 31, 124, 1980
C. Lane. *The Burdens of Intimacy: Psychoanalysis and Victorian Masculinity*, Chicago University Press, 1999
R. Langbaum. *Thomas Hardy in Our Time*, Palgrave Macmillan, London, 1997
Elizabeth Langland. "A Perspective of One's Own: Thomas Hardy and the Elusive Sue Bridehead", *Studies in the Novel*, 12, 1980
—. *Gothic Manners and the Classic English Novel*, University of Wisconsin Press, Madison, 1988
—. "Masculinity in *Jude the Obscure*", in M. Higonnet, 1993
Albert J. LaValley, ed. *Tess of the D'Urbervilles: A Collection of Critical Essays*, Prentice-Hall, New Jersey, 1969
J. Law. "'A Passing Corporeal Blight': Political Bodies in *Tess of the d'Urbervilles*", *Victorian Studies*, 40, 2, 1997
D.H. Lawrence. *Study of Thomas Hardy and Other Essays*, ed. Bruce Steele, Cambridge University Press, 1985
—. *A Selection from Phoenix*, ed. A.A.H. Inglis, Penguin, 1971
—. *Selected Essays*, Penguin, 1950
—. *The Rainbow*, ed. John Worthen, Penguin, 1981/6
—. *The Complete Short Novels*, ed. Keith Sagar & Melissa Partridge, Penguin, 1982/7
—. *Aaron's Rod*, Penguin, 1950
—. *Sons and Lovers*, ed. Keith Sagar, Penguin, 1981/6
—. *Kangaroo*, Penguin, 1950
Herman Lea. *Thomas Hardy's Wessex*, Macmillan, London, 1977
Glenda Leeming. *Who's Who in Thomas Hardy*, Elm Tree, 1975
Lawrence Lerner & John Holmstrom. *Thomas Hardy and His Readers*, Bodley Head, 1968
S. Lee. "An Essay on Tess's Androgynous Vision: Hardy's Yin-Yang Principle in *Tess of the d'Urbervilles*", *Journal of English Language and Literature*, 35, 4, 1989
P. Lennon,. "*Tess* on the American Stage", *The Thomas Hardy Journal*, 7, 3, 1991
J. LeVay. "Hardy's *Jude the Obscure*", *Explicator*, 49:4, 1991
Charles Lock. *Thomas Hardy: Criticism in Focus*, Bristol Classic Press, 1992

David Lodge. *Language of Fiction,* Routledge & Kegan Paul, 1966
Bryan Longhrey, ed. *Critical Survey,* Thomas Hardy number, 5, 2, 1983
Jakob Lothe. "Hardy's Authorial Narrative Methods in *Tess of the d'Urbervilles*", in J. Hawthorn, 1986
John Lucas. *The Literature of Change,* Harvester, 1977
Christobel Mackenzie: "The Anti-Sexism Campaign Invites You to Fight Sexism, Not Sex", in A. Assiter, 1993
S. Maier. *Tess of the d'Urbervilles/ Thomas Hardy,* Broadview, Peterborough, 1996
—. *Tess of the d'Urbervilles: A Pure Woman Faithfully Presented,* Peterborough, Broadview, 2007
Phillip V. Mallett & Ronald P. Draper, eds. *A Spacious Vision: Essays on Hardy,* Patten Press, Penzance, 1994
—. "Sexual Ideology and Narrative Form in *Jude the Obscure*", *English,* 38:162, 1989
—. *The Achievement of Thomas Hardy,* Palgrave Macmillan, 2000
—. ed. *Thomas Hardy: Texts and Contexts,* Palgrave Macmillan, London, 2002
P. Manzer. "'In Some Old Book, Somebody Just Like Me': Eliot's *Tess* and Hardy's *Tess*", *English Language Notes,* 33, 3, 1996
Jane Marcus. "A Tess For Child Molesters", *Jump Cut,* 3, 1981
Elaine Marks & Isabelle de Courtivron, eds. *New French Feminisms: an anthology,* Harvester Wheatsheaf, 1981
K. Marsden. *The Poems of Thomas Hardy: A Critical Introduction,* London, 1969
Karl Marx, *Selected Works,* I, Lawrence & Wishart, 1942
K. Maynard. *Thomas Hardy's Tragic Poetry,* University of Iowa Press, 1991
S. McEathron. *Thomas Hardy's Tess of the d'Urbervilles: A Sourcebook,* New York, NY: Routledge, 2005
L. McQuiston. *Suffragettes to She-Devils: Women's Liberation and Beyond,* Phaidon, London, 1997
R. McRuer. *The Queer Renaissance,* New York University Press, New York, NY, 1997
E. Michie. "Dressing Up: Hardy's *Tess of the d'Urbervilles* and Oliphant's *Phoebe Junior*", *Victorian Literature and Culture,* 30, 1, 2002
Helena Michie. *The Flesh Made Word: Female Figures and Women's Bodies,* Oxford University Press, 1987
Ruth Milberg-Kaye. *Thomas Hardy: Myths of Sexuality,* John Jay Press, New York, NY, 1983
R. Miles. "The Women of Wessex", in A. Smith, 1979
J. Hillis Miller. *Thomas Hardy: Distance and Desire,* Oxford University Press, 1970
—. *Fiction and Repetition: Seven English Novels,* Harvard University Press, 1982
Kate Millett. *Sexual Politics,* Doubleday, Garden City, 1970
Michael Millgate. *Thomas Hardy: His Career as a Novelist,* Bodley Head, 1971
—. *Thomas Hardy: A Biography,* Oxford University Press, 1982
—. *Thomas Hardy: A Biography Revisited,* Oxford University Press, 2004
Sara Mills, ed: *Gendering the Reader,* Harvester Wheatsheaf, 1993
W. Mitsichelli. "Androgyny, Survival, and Fulfilment in Thomas Hardy's *Far From the Madding Crowd*", *Modern Language Studies,* 18, 3, 1988
E. Moers. *New York Review of Books,* Nov 9, 1967
Toril Moi. *Sexual/Textual Politics: Feminist Literary Theory,* Routledge, 1988
—. ed. *French Feminist Thought,* Blackwell, 1988
Rosemarie Morgan. *Women and Sexuality in the Novels of Thomas Hardy,* Routledge, 1988

—. *Cancelled Words: Rediscovering Thomas Hardy*, Routledge, 1992
—. *Student Companion to Thomas Hardy*, Greenwood Publishing Group, 2007
Roy Morrell. *Thomas Hardy: The Will and the Way*, University of Malaysia Press, 1965
R.D. Morrison. "Reading and Restoration in *Tess of the d'Urbervilles*", *Victorian Newsletter*, 82, 1992
Sally Munt, ed. *New Lesbian Criticism: Literary and Cultural Readings*, Harvester Wheatsheaf, 1992
D. Musselwhite. *Social Transformations in Hardy's Tragic Novels: Megamachines and Phantasms*, Basingstoke, Palgrave Macmillan, 2003
—. "*Tess of the d'Urbervilles*: 'a Becoming Woman'; or, Deleuze and Guattari Go to Wessex", *Textual Practice*, 14, 3, 2000
J. Mustafa. "'A Good Horror Has Its Place in Art': Hardy's Gothic Strategy in *Tess of the d'Urbervilles*", *Studies in the Humanities*, 32.2, 2005
M. Myer, Michael Grosvenor. "'Traditional' Lullabies in Victorian Fiction: *Wuthering Heights* and *Tess of the d'Urbervilles*", *Notes and Queries*, 35, 1988
T. Nash. "*Tess of the d'Urbervilles*: The Symbolic Use of Folklore", *English Language Notes*, 35, 4, 1998
Lynda Nead. *Female Nude: Art, Obscenity and Sexuality*, Routledge, 1992
E. Neill. *Trial by Ordeal: Thomas Hardy and the Critics*, Camden House, 1999
—. *The Secret Life of Thomas Hardy*, Ashgate Publishing, 2004
Paul J. Niemeyer. *Seeing Hardy: Film and Television Adaptations of the Fiction of Thomas Hardy*, McFarland & Co., 2003
S. Nishimura. "Language, Violence, and Irrevocability: Speech Acts in *Tess of the d'Urbervilles*", *Studies in the Novel*, 37, 2
H. Orel. *The Final Years of Thomas Hardy 1912-1928*, London, 1976
—. *Thomas Hardy's Epic Drama: A Study of 'The Dynasts*, Kansas, 1963
Timothy O'Sullivan. *Thomas Hardy: An Illustrated Biography*, Macmillan, London, 1981
L. Otis,. "Organic Memory: History, Bodies and Texts in *Tess of the d'Urbervilles*", *Nineteenth-Century Studies*, 8, 1994
T. O'Toole. *Genealogy and Fiction in Hardy*, Palgrave Macmillan, London, 1997
K. Padian,. "'A Daughter of the Soil': Themes of Deep Time and Evolution in Thomas Hardy's *Tess of the d'Urbervilles*", *Thomas Hardy Journal*, 13, 3, 1997
Norman Page, ed. *Thomas Hardy: The Writer and His Background*, Bell & Hyman, 1980
—. ed. *Thomas Hardy Annual*, Macmillan, London, 1983-
—. & Peter Preston, eds. *The Literature of Place*, Macmillan, London, 1993
—. *Thomas Hardy: Family History*, Routledge/ Thoemmes Press, 1998
—. ed. *The Oxford Reader's Companion to Hardy*, Oxford University Press, Oxford, 2000
—. *Thomas Hardy: The Novels*, Palgrave MacMillan, 2001
B. Paris. ""A Confusion of Many Standards": Conflicting Value Systems in *Tess of the d'Urbervilles*", *Nineteenth Century Fiction*, 24, 1970
Lynn Parker. ""Pure Woman" and Tragic Heroine? Conflicting Myths in Hardy's *Tess of the d'Urbervilles*", *Studies in the Novel*, 24, 1992
J. Paterson. "*The Return of the Native* as Antichristian Document", *NineteenthCentury Fiction*, 14, 1959
—. *The Making of 'The Return of the Native'*, University of California Press, 1960
M. Patil. *Thomas Hardy, the Poet*, Atlantic Publishers, 1998
Michael Payne. *Reading Theory: An Introduction to Lacan, Derrida, and Kristeva*,

Blackwell, 1993
John Peck. *How to Study a Thomas Hardy Novel*, Macmillan, London, 1983
Charles P.C. Petit, ed. *New Perspectives on Thomas Hardy*, Macmillan, London, 1994
—. ed. *Reading Thomas Hardy*, Palgrave Macmillan, London, 1998
F.B. Pinion. *A Hardy Companion*, Macmillan, London, 1968
—. ed. *Thomas Hardy and the Modern World*, Thomas Hardy Society, Dorchester, 1974
—. *Thomas Hardy: Art and Thought*, Macmillan, London, 1977
—. ed. *A Thomas Hardy Dictionary*, Palgrave Macmillan, 1992
Ralph Pite. *Thomas Hardy: The Guarded Life*, Picador, 2006
Monique Plaza. ""Phallomorphic power" and the psychology of "woman"", *Ideology and Consciousness*, 4, 1978
Birgit Plietzsch. *The Novels of Thomas Hardy as a Product of Nineteenth-Century Social, Economic, and Cultural Change*, Tenea Verlag, 2004
M. Ponsford. "Thomas Hardy's Control of Sympathy in *Tess of the D'Urbervilles*", *Midwest Quarterly*, 27:4, 1986
Adrian Poole. "Men's Words and Hardy's Women", *Essays in Criticism*, 31, 1981
C.L. Preston. *A KWIC Concordance to Thomas Hardy's Tess of the d'Urbervilles*, Garland, New York, NY, 1989
R.L. Purdy. *Thomas Hardy: A Bibliography Study*, Oxford University Press, 1954
Lyn Pykett. "Ruinous bodies: women and sexuality in Hardy's late fiction", in B. Longhrey, 1983
John Rabbets. *From Hardy to Faulkner: Wessex to Yoknapatawpha*, Macmillan, London, 1989
A. Radford. "The Making of a Goddess: Hardy, Lawrence and Persephone", *Connotations: A Journal for Critical Debate*, 12, 2-3, 2002
—. *Thomas Hardy and the Survivals of Time*, Ashgate Publishing, 2003
—. "Lost Girls in Hardy and Lawrence", *Southern Humanities Review*, 38, 3, 2004
H. Radner. *Shopping Around: Feminine Culture and the Pursuit of Pleasure*, Routledge, New York, NY, 1995
P. Ralph. *Hardy's Geography*, Palgrave Macmillan, London, 2002
M. Ray. *An Annotated Critical Bibliography of Thomas Hardy*, London, 1989
—. *Thomas Hardy*, Ashgate, Aldershot, 1997
Philip Rice & Patricia Waugh, eds. *Modern Literary Theory: A Reader*, Arnold 1992
Adrienne Rich. *Blood, Bread and Poetry*, Virago, 1980
—. *Of Woman Born: Motherhood as Experience and Institution*, Virago, 1977
J. Riquelme, ed. *Tess of the d'Urbervilles: Complete, Authoritative Text with Biographical and Historical Contexts, Critical History, and Essays from Five Contemporary Critical Perspectives* Boston, MA: Bedford, 1998
Jeanne Addison Roberts. *The Shakespearean Wild: Geography, Genus and Gender*, University of Nebraska Press, Lincoln, Nebraska 1991
Katherine Rogers. "Women in Thomas Hardy", *Centennial Review*, 19, 1975
E. Rooney. "'A Little More Than Persuading': Tess and the Subject of Sexual Violence", in *Rape and Representation*, eds. Lynn A. Higgins & Brenda R. Silver: Columbia University Press, New York, 1991
Becky Rosa: "Anti-monogamy: A Radical Challenge to Compulsory Heterosexuality?", in G. Griffin, 1994
P. Roy. "Agent or Victim: Thomas Hardy's *Tess of the d'Urbervilles*, 1891," *Women in Literature: Reading through the Lens of Gender*, eds. Jerilyn Fisher *et al*, Greenwood, Westport, CT, 2003

D. Sadoff: "Looking at Tess: The Female Figure in Two Narrative Media", in M. Higonnet, 1993

R. Saldivar. "*Jude the Obscure*: Reading and the Spirit of the Law", *English Literary History*, 50:3, 1983

C.H. Salter. *Good Little Thomas Hardy*, Macmillan, London, 1981

B. Santangelo. "A Moral Dilemma: Ethics in *Tess of the D'Urbervilles*", *English Studies*, 75:1, 1994

J. Schad. *Victorians in Theory From Derrida to Browning*, Manchester University Press, 1999

Nadine Schoenburg. "The Supernatural in *Tess*", *Thomas Hardy Yearbook*, 19, 1989

Arthur Schopenhauer. *Essays and Aphorisms*, Penguin, 1970

Julie Sherrick. *Thomas Hardy's Major Novels*, Rowman & Littlefield, 1998

J. Shumaker. "Breaking with the Conventions: Victorian Confession Novels and *Tess of the D'Urbervilles*", *English Literature in Transition (1880-1920)*, 37:4, 1994

Robert Schweik, "Moral Perspective in *Tess of the D'Urbervilles*", *College English*, 24, 1962

—. "Theme, Character and Perspective in Hardy's *The Return of the Native*", *Philological Quarterly*, 41, 1962

Janie Sénèchal. "Focalisation, Regard et Désire dans *Far From the Madding Crowd*," *Cahiers Victoriens et Edouardiens*, 12, 1980

Martin Seymour-Smith. *Hardy*, Bloomsbury, 1995

Charles Shapiro, ed. *Twelve Original Essays on Great English Novels*, Detroit 1960

G.W. Sherman. *The Pessimism of Thomas Hardy*, Associated University Press, New Jersey, 1976

J. Sherrick. *Thomas Hardy's Major Novels*, Scarecrow Press, 1998

Elaine Showalter, ed. *The New Feminist Criticism*, Virago 1986

Kaja Silverman. "History, Figuration and Female Subjectivity in *Tess of the d'Urbervilles*", *Novel*, 18, 1984

—. *The Acoustic Mirror: The Female Voice in Psychoanalysis and Cinema*, Indiana University Press, Bloomington, 1988

A. Simpson, Anne B. "Sue Bridehead Revisited", *Victorian Literature and Culture*, 19, 1991

Anne Smith, ed. *The Novels of Thomas Hardy*, Vision Press, 1979

J. Smith & C. Ferstman. *The Castration of Oedipus: Feminism, Psychopanalysis and the Will to Power*, New York University Press, 1996

J. Sommers. "Hardy's other *Bildungsroman: Tess*", *English Literature in Transition*, 25, 1982

David Sonstroem. "Order and Disorder in *Jude the Obscure*", *English Literature in Transition*, 24, 1981

F.R. Southerington. *Hardy's Vision of Man*, Chatto & Windus, 1971

Dale Spender. *The Writing or the Sex? Why you don't have to read women's writing to know it's no good*, Pergamon Press, New York, NY, 1989

Marlene Springer. *Hardy's Use of Allusion*, Macmillan, London, 1983

R.W. Stallamn. "Hardy's Hour-Glass Novel", *Sewanee Review*, 55, 1947

H. Stevens & C. Howlett, eds. *Modernist Sexualities*, Manchester University Press, 2000

P. Stiles,. "Grace, Redemption and the 'Fallen Woman': *Ruth* and *Tess of the d'Urbervilles*", *Gaskell Society Journal*, 6, 1992

J. Strong, Jeremy. "*Tess, Jude*, and the Problem of Adapting Hardy", *Literature/Film*

Quarterly, 34, 3, 2006

Patricia Stubbs. *Women and Fiction: Feminism and the Novel, 1880-1920*, Harvester, 1979

Rosemary Sumner. *Thomas Hardy: Psychological Novelist*, Macmillan, London, 1981

B. Szumzki. *Readings on Tess of the d'Urbervilles*, San Diego, CA: Greenhaven, 2000

T. Tanner. "Colour and Movement in Hardy's *Tess of the d'Urbervilles*", *Critical Quarterly*, 10, 1968

Dennis Taylor. *Hardy's Poetry, 1860-1928*, Macmillan, London, 1981

—. "The Second Hardy", *Sewanee Review*, 96, 1988

—. *Hardy's Metres and Victorian Prosody*, Oxford, 1988

Richard H. Taylor. *The Neglected Hardy*, Macmillan, London, 1982

J. Thomas. *Thomas Hardy, Femininity and Dissent*, Palgrave Macmillan, London, 1998

Charlotte Thompson. "Language and the Shape of Reality in *Tess of the d'Urbervilles*", *English Literary History*, 50, 4, 1983

G. Thurley. *The Psychology of Hardy's Novels*, St Lucia, 1975

Claire Tomalin. *Thomas Hardy*, Penguin Press, 2007

S. Trezise. "Places in Time: Discovering the Chronotope in *Tess of the D'Urbervilles*", *Critical Survey*, 5:2, 1993

Eric Tridgill. *Madonnas and Magdalens: The Origins and Development of Victorian Sexual Attitudes*, Heinemann, 1976

P. Turner. *The Life of Thomas Hardy*, Blackwell, Oxford, 2001

G. Veidemanis. "*Tess of the D'Urbervilles*: What the Film Left Out", *English Journal*, 77:7, 1988

Christopher Walbank. *Thomas Hardy*, Blackie, Glasgow, 1979

C.C. Walcutt. "Character and Coincidence in *The Return of the Native*", in C. Shapiro, 1960

Nell K. Waldman. ""All that she is": Hardy's Tess and Polanski's", *Queen'sQuarterly*, 88, 3, 1981

U. Walters. *The Poetry of Thomas Hardy's Novels*, Edwin Mellen Press, 1980

Marina Warner. *Alone Of All Her Sex: The Myth and Cult of the Virgin Mary*, Picador 1985

C. Watts. "Hardy's Sue Bridehead and the 'New Woman'", *Critical Survey*, 5:2, 1993

Valerie Wayne, ed. *The Matter of Difference: Materialist Feminist Criticism of Shakespeare*, Harvester Wheatsheaf, 1991

Harvey Webster. *On a Darkling Plain*, University of California Press, 1947

R. Webster. "Reproducing Hardy: Familiar and Unfamiliar Versions of *Far from the Madding Crowd* and *Tess of the D'Urbervilles*", *Critical Survey*, 5:2, 1993

—. "The Novels of Thomas Hardy: Tess of the d'Urbervilles", in *Literature in Context*, eds. Rick Rylance and Judy Simons: Palgrave, Basingstoke 2001

Judith Weissman. "The Deceased Wife's Sister Marriage Act and the Ending of *Tess of the d'Urbervilles*", *American Notes and Queries*, 14, 1976

Ottis Wheeler. "Four Versions of *The Return of the Native*", *Nineteenth Century Fiction*, 14, 1959

R.J. White. *Thomas Hardy and History*, Macmillan, London, 1974

Margaret Whitford. *Luce Irigaray: Philosophy in the Feminine*, Routledge, 1991

G. Glen Wickens. "Victorian Theories of Language and *Tess of the d'Urbervilles*", *Mosaic*, 19, 1986

—. "Hardy and the Aesthetic Mythographers: The Myth of Demeter and Persephone in *Tess of the d'Urbervilles*", *University of Toronto Quarterly*, 53, 1, 1983

—. "'Sermons in Stones': The Return to Nature in *Tess of the d'Urbervilles*", *English Studies in Canada*, 14, 2, 1988
Peter Widdowson. *Hardy in History: A study in literary sociology*, Routledge, 1989
—. *D.H. Lawrence*, Longman, 1992
—. ed. *Thomas Hardy: Tess of the d'Urbervilles: New Casebooks*, Macmillan, London, 1993
—. ed. *Thomas Hardy*, Palgrave Macmillan, London, 1996
Jonathan Wike. "The World as Text in Hardy's Fiction", *Nineteenth Century Literature*, 47, 1993
Linda Ruth Williams. *Critical Desire: Psychoanalysis and the Literary Subject*, Arnold, 1995
—. *Sex in the Head*, Harvester Wheatsheaf, 1995
—. *D.H. Lawrence, Writers and Their Works*, Northcote House, 1997
Merryn Williams. *Thomas Hardy and Rural England*, Macmillan, London, 1972
—. *A Preface to Hardy*, Longman, 1976
M. Williams. "'Sensitive as Gossamer'-Law and Sexual Encounter in *Tess of the d'Urbervilles*", *Thomas Hardy Journal*, 17, 1, 2001
K. Wilson. *Thomas Hardy on Stage*, Palgrave Macmillan, London, 1994
George Wing. *Hardy*, Oliver & Boyd, 1963
—. "Theme and Fancy in Hardy's *The Well-Beloved*", *Dalhouse Review*, 56, 1977
T. Winnifrith. *Fallen Women In the 19th Century Novel*, Macmillan, 1993
Judith Wittenberg. "Angels of Vision and Questions of Gender in *Far From the Madding Crowd*", *The Centennial Review*, 31, 1, 1968
—. "Thomas Hardy's First Novel: Women and the Quest for Autonomy", *Colby Library Quarterly*, 18, 1982
—. "Early Hardy Novels and the Fictional Eye", *Novel*, 16, 1983
Monique Wittig. *The Lesbian Body*, tr. David Le Vay, Beacon Press, Boston 1986
—. *The Straight Mind*, Beacon Press, Boston, 1992
J. Wolmark, ed. *Cybersexualities: A Reader on Feminist Theory, Cyborgs and Cyberspace*, Edinburgh University Press, 1999
T. Woods. *Beginning Postmodernism*, Manchester University Press, Manchester, 1999
V. Woolf. *The Second Common Reader*, New York, 1932
George Wootton. *Thomas Hardy: Towards a Materialist Criticism*, Barnes & Noble, Goldenbridge, 1985
E. Wright, ed. *Feminism and Psychoanalysis: A Critical Dictionary*, Blackwell, 1992
Sarah Bird Wright. *Thomas Hardy A to Z: The Essential Reference to His Life and Work*, Facts on File, 2002
Terence Wright. *Tess of the d'Urbervilles*, Macmillan, London, 1987
—. *Hardy and the Erotic*, Macmillan, London, 1989
—. "Space, Time, and Paradox: The Sense of History in Hardy's Last Novels", in A. Easson, ed. *History and the Novel, Essays and Studies*, 44, Brewer, Cambridge, 1991
—. *Hardy and His Readers*, Macmillan, 2003
—. *Thomas Hardy on Screen*, Cambridge University Press, Cambridge, 2005
P. Zietlow. *Moments of Vision: The Poetry of Thomas Hardy*, Cambridge, MA, 1974
M. Ziaja-Buchholtz. "In Search of the Lost Genre: The Tragic Dimension of Thomas Hardy's *Tess of the d'Urbervilles*", *Lubelskie Materiały Neofilologiczne*, 22, 1998
Jack Zipes. *Don't Bet on the Prince: Contemporary Feminist Fairy Tales in North America and England*, Methuen, New York, NY, 1986

WEBSITES

hardysociety.org
st-andrews.ac.uk/ttha
neal.oxborrow.net/Thomas_Hardy

CRESCENT MOON PUBLISHING

ARTS, PAINTING, SCULPTURE

The Art of Andy Goldsworthy: Complete Works
Andy Goldsworthy: Touching Nature
Andy Goldsworthy in Close-Up
Andy Goldsworthy: Pocket Guide
Andy Goldsworthy In America
Land Art: A Complete Guide
The Art of Richard Long: Complete Works
Richard Long: Pocket Guide
Land Art In the UK
Land Art in Close-Up
Land Art In the U.S.A.
Land Art: Pocket Guide
Installation Art in Close-Up
Minimal Art and Artists In the 1960s and After
Colourfield Painting
Land Art DVD, TV documentary
Andy Goldsworthy DVD, TV documentary
The Erotic Object: Sexuality in Sculpture From Prehistory to the Present Day
Sex in Art: Pornography and Pleasure in Painting and Sculpture
Postwar Art
Sacred Gardens: The Garden in Myth, Religion and Art
Glorification: Religious Abstraction in Renaissance and 20th Century Art
Early Netherlandish Painting
Leonardo da Vinci
Piero della Francesca
Giovanni Bellini
Fra Angelico: Art and Religion in the Renaissance
Mark Rothko: The Art of Transcendence
Frank Stella: American Abstract Artist
Jasper Johns
Brice Marden
Alison Wilding: The Embrace of Sculpture
Vincent van Gogh: Visionary Landscapes
Eric Gill: Nuptials of God
Constantin Brancusi: Sculpting the Essence of Things
Max Beckmann
Caravaggio
Gustave Moreau
Egon Schiele: Sex and Death In Purple Stockings
Delizioso Fotografico Fervore: Works In Process 1
Sacro Cuore: Works In Process 2
The Light Eternal: J.M.W. Turner
The Madonna Glorified: Karen Arthurs

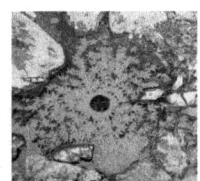

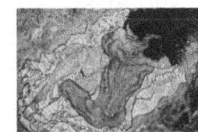

LITERATURE

J.R.R. Tolkien: The Books, The Films, The Whole Cultural Phenomenon
J.R.R. Tolkien: Pocket Guide
Tolkien's Heroic Quest
The *Earthsea* Books of Ursula Le Guin
Beauties, Beasts and Enchantment: Classic French Fairy Tales
German Popular Tales by the Brothers Grimm
Philip Ullman and *His Dark Materials*
Sexing Hardy: Thomas Hardy and Feminism
Thomas Hardy's *Tess of the d'Urbervilles*
Thomas Hardy's *Jude the Obscure*
Thomas Hardy: The Tragic Novels
Love and Tragedy: Thomas Hardy
The Poetry of Landscape in Hardy
Wessex Revisited: Thomas Hardy and John Cowper Powys
Wolfgang Iser: Essays and Interviews
Petrarch, Dante and the Troubadours
Maurice Sendak and the Art of Children's Book Illustration
Andrea Dworkin
Cixous, Irigaray, Kristeva: The *Jouissance* of French Feminism
Julia Kristeva: Art, Love, Melancholy, Philosophy, Semiotics and Psychoanalysis
Hélène Cixous I Love You: The *Jouissance* of Writing
Luce Irigaray: Lips, Kissing, and the Politics of Sexual Difference
Peter Redgrove: Here Comes the Flood
Peter Redgrove: Sex-Magic-Poetry-Cornwall
Lawrence Durrell: Between Love and Death, East and West
Love, Culture & Poetry: Lawrence Durrell
Cavafy: Anatomy of a Soul
German Romantic Poetry: Goethe, Novalis, Heine, Hölderlin
Feminism and Shakespeare
Shakespeare: Love, Poetry & Magic
The Passion of D.H. Lawrence
D.H. Lawrence: Symbolic Landscapes
D.H. Lawrence: Infinite Sensual Violence
Rimbaud: Arthur Rimbaud and the Magic of Poetry
The Ecstasies of John Cowper Powys
Sensualism and Mythology: The Wessex Novels of John Cowper Powys
Amorous Life: John Cowper Powys and the Manifestation of Affectivity (H.W. Fawkner)
Postmodern Powys: New Essays on John Cowper Powys (Joe Boulter)
Rethinking Powys: Critical Essays on John Cowper Powys
Paul Bowles & Bernardo Bertolucci
Rainer Maria Rilke
Joseph Conrad: *Heart of Darkness*
In the Dim Void: Samuel Beckett
Samuel Beckett Goes into the Silence
André Gide: Fiction and Fervour
Jackie Collins and the Blockbuster Novel
Blinded By Her Light: The Love-Poetry of Robert Graves
The Passion of Colours: Travels In Mediterranean Lands
Poetic Forms

POETRY

Ursula Le Guin: Walking In Cornwall
Peter Redgrove: Here Comes The Flood
Peter Redgrove: Sex-Magic-Poetry-Cornwall
Dante: Selections From the *Vita Nuova*
Petrarch, Dante and the Troubadours
William Shakespeare: *The Sonnets*
William Shakespeare: Complete Poems
Blinded By Her Light: The Love-Poetry of Robert Graves
Emily Dickinson: Selected Poems
Emily Brontë: Poems
Thomas Hardy: Selected Poems
Percy Bysshe Shelley: Poems
John Keats: Selected Poems
D.H. Lawrence: Selected Poems
Edmund Spenser: Poems
Edmund Spenser: *Amoretti*
John Donne: Poems
Henry Vaughan: Poems
Sir Thomas Wyatt: Poems
Robert Herrick: Selected Poems
Rilke: Space, Essence and Angels in the Poetry of Rainer Maria Rilke
Rainer Maria Rilke: Selected Poems
Friedrich Hölderlin: Selected Poems
Arseny Tarkovsky: Selected Poems
Novalis: *Hymns To the Night*
Paul Verlaine: Selected Poems
Arthur Rimbaud: Selected Poems
Arthur Rimbaud: *A Season in Hell*
Arthur Rimbaud and the Magic of Poetry
D.J. Enright: By-Blows
Jeremy Reed: Brigitte's Blue Heart
Jeremy Reed: Claudia Schiffer's Red Shoes
Gorgeous Little Orpheus
Radiance: New Poems
Crescent Moon Book of Nature Poetry
Crescent Moon Book of Love Poetry
Crescent Moon Book of Mystical Poetry
Crescent Moon Book of Elizabethan Love Poetry
Crescent Moon Book of Metaphysical Poetry
Crescent Moon Book of Romantic Poetry
Pagan America: New American Poetry

MEDIA, CINEMA, FEMINISM and CULTURAL STUDIES

J.R.R. Tolkien: The Books, The Films, The Whole Cultural Phenomenon
J.R.R. Tolkien: Pocket Guide
The *Lord of the Rings* Movies: Pocket Guide
The Cinema of Hayao Miyazaki
Hayao Miyazaki: *Princess Mononoke*: Pocket Movie Guide
Hayao Miyazaki: *Spirited Away*: Pocket Movie Guide
Tim Burton
Ken Russell
Ken Russell: *Tommy*: Pocket Movie Guide
The Ghost Dance: The Origins of Religion
The Peyote Cult
Cixous, Irigaray, Kristeva: The *Jouissance* of French Feminism
Julia Kristeva: Art, Love, Melancholy, Philosophy, Semiotics and Psychoanalysis
Luce Irigaray: Lips, Kissing, and the Politics of Sexual Difference
Hélène Cixous I Love You: The *Jouissance* of Writing
Andrea Dworkin
'Cosmo Woman': The World of Women's Magazines
Women in Pop Music
Discovering the Goddess (Geoffrey Ashe)
The Poetry of Cinema
The Sacred Cinema of Andrei Tarkovsky
Andrei Tarkovsky: Pocket Guide
Andrei Tarkovsky: *Mirror*: Pocket Movie Guide
Andrei Tarkovsky: *The Sacrifice*: Pocket Movie Guide
Walerian Borowczyk: Cinema of Erotic Dreams
Jean-Luc Godard: The Passion of Cinema
Jean-Luc Godard: *Hail Mary*: Pocket Movie Guide
Jean-Luc Godard: *Contempt*: Pocket Movie Guide
Jean-Luc Godard: *Pierrot le Fou*: Pocket Movie Guide
John Hughes and Eighties Cinema
Ferris Bueller's Day Off: Pocket Movie Guide
Jean-Luc Godard: Pocket Guide
The Cinema of Richard Linklater
Liv Tyler: Star In Ascendance
Blade Runner and the Films of Philip K. Dick
Paul Bowles and Bernardo Bertolucci
Media Hell: Radio, TV and the Press
An Open Letter to the BBC
Detonation Britain: Nuclear War in the UK
Feminism and Shakespeare
Wild Zones: Pornography, Art and Feminism
Sex in Art: Pornography and Pleasure in Painting and Sculpture
Sexing Hardy: Thomas Hardy and Feminism

In my view *The Light Eternal* is among the very best of all the material I read on Turner. (Douglas Graham, director of the Turner Museum, Denver, Colorado)

The Light Eternal is a model monograph, an exemplary job. The subject matter of the book is beautifully organised and dead on beam. (Lawrence Durrell)

It is amazing for me to see my work treated with such passion and respect. (Andrea Dworkin)

CRESCENT MOON PUBLISHING
P.O. Box 1312, Maidstone, Kent, ME14 5XU, Great Britain. www.crmoon.com

www.ingramcontent.com/pod-product-compliance
Lightning Source LLC
Chambersburg PA
CBHW070048100426
42734CB00040B/2739